A Young Person's Guide to the Ballet

Including interviews with Lynn Seymour *and* George de la Pena

A Young Person's Guide to the Ballet

Craig Dodd

Macdonald General Books
Macdonald and Jane's
London and Sydney

Designed and produced by Breslich & Foss
25 Lloyd Baker Street, London WC1X 9AT

Designer: Harold Bartram

First published in 1980 by Macdonald General Books,
Macdonald and Jane's Publishing Group Ltd
Paulton House, 8 Shepherdess Walk, London N1 7LW

Printed in Great Britain
by W & J Mackay Limited, Chatham

ISBN 0 354 04499 0

Contents

The Birth of the Ballet

What picture comes to mind when you hear the word 'ballet'? Is it a long line of ballerinas in short *tutus* moving across the stage as Swans, or the exciting, dramatic dancing of the brilliant male dancers of today? Or do you think of a ballerina, her hair drawn tightly back, wearing a long white tulle skirt with tight bodice and perhaps a pair of transparent wings? If the latter is your image, you are thinking of ballet almost as it was when it first became a theatre art one hundred and fifty years ago.

Of course many forms of dance existed long before then. Think how many colourful folk dances there are, ranging from English maypole dances to oriental temple dancing. The fiery dancers of Georgia in Russia danced on their toes long before ballet was born, although these flamboyant steps were only performed by the men. Folk dances, carefully handed down from generation to generation, are performed by ordinary people and usually require no special technique. Ballet, on the other hand, is artificial and grew out of stately court dances whose steps were arranged (choreographed) by ballet masters for the court. Gradually the styles and patterns produced were written down and carefully practised until they became so specialized that only highly trained dancers could do them.

To understand ballet, and especially a ballet performance, you do not need to know the history of dance at court before it became dance in the theatre, but it is a fascinating story. Dance was an important part of court life, not just a light entertainment. It even played its part in politics, and kings and princes would arrange extravagant displays by entertainers to impress visiting ambassadors. They would cleverly arrange for flattering

---

On title page
Adam Luders, a principal dancer of the New York City Ballet.

Opposite
A scene from the *Ballet Comique de la Reine* which shows the arrangement of designs, performers, audience and guests.

or threatening hints to be put into the dances so that the visitors would know their intentions.

These entertainments were not performances as we know them today, for the whole court, including the monarch, would often take part. When he appeared, he would always lead the dance with the court ranged around him in strict order of precedence. Sometimes the king or queen would dance for simple pleasure—Elizabeth I of England much enjoyed a jig—or on other occasions the monarch would play a leading role. In fact Louis XIV of France is remembered by the title of his greatest role, that of the Sun King.

The word 'ballet' comes from the Italian words *ballo*, a dance, and *balletto*, a little dance. As you will know if you study ballet, the words for the steps and positions are in French, because although dancing began in Italy, it was developed in France. During the fifteenth and sixteenth centuries, the Italy we know today was a collection of small states. In these courts the first great spectacles took place and it was an Italian, Catherine de Medici, who later took the art to France, when she became Henry II's queen.

In France Catherine employed the famous violinist and ballet master, Beaujoyeulx—up to recent times it was the practice for the violin to be used for the ballet class and not the piano which is used today. Her greatest achievement was an entertainment, given in 1581, to celebrate the wedding of one of her relatives. This performance was beautifully recorded in a book and it is from these illustrations that we can work out what these entertainments were like. We can see that the action took place over the whole banqueting area, with the visitors seated on a raised platform at one end of the hall and courtiers, who were not taking part, in upper galleries around the side. Apart from showing the importance of the guests, this raised platform would enable them to see the complicated patterns the dancers would make as they moved to and fro across the floor. The dances of this period were usually arranged for large groups and not for individual dancers. In these early years quick steps or even little jumps were unknown, and often the main characters did not move at all, but would stand in some suitable pose on a decorated chariot which might be pulled around.

The stories of these dances were usually taken from classical Greek or

Opposite
Louis XIV as the Sun King, his greatest role.

Below
Ballet du Noel des Fleurs of 1618 shows how dancers in the palace courtyard were spaced to make attractive patterns.

This painting by Lancret of Marie-Anne de Cupis de Camargo is to be found in most books about ballet. Different versions exist in art galleries in Britain and America, but all show the same details: the hint of ankle revealed by her shortened skirt and the musicians taking notice of it.

Roman stories and, as in the very first banquets, might be chosen as suitable accompaniment for each course. For example, a big roast might be presented with the goddess of the hunt, Diana, and her attendants.

The ability to dance was an important skill at court, and courtiers practised and perfected the movements in order to look more graceful. During the reign of Louis XIV, in the seventeenth century, it was considered absolutely necessary to have these skills, for the King himself was an outstanding performer, and had been since a child. He employed the most famous and talented musicians and ballet masters of the day to create displays and he often took the leading parts himself. Altogether he took dancing very seriously indeed, so seriously that he decided to set up an academy to bring together the best teachers of the day to organize dance on a proper basis. Ten years later this institution had become a school for arranging performances and today, nearly three hundred and twenty years later, it is still in operation as the Paris Opéra.

As Louis grew older and fatter, and could no longer dance with his

Ondine was one of the ballets created during the Romantic period about supernatural beings. The original has been long forgotten, but Sir Frederick Ashton created a beautiful version for Dame Margot Fonteyn and Heinz Spoerhli created one for his ballerina, Maria Guerrero, in Basle, Switzerland (above). Both used a modern score by Hans Werner Henze in place of the original by Pugni.

usual brilliance, he stopped performing. This simple act marks the beginning of dance as an occupation for professional dancers, for as soon as the King stopped, the courtiers had to stop as well. Instead of being performers, they became the audience.

By this time there already were professional dancers, but these would mostly take part in mime plays or popular entertainments and might be thought of as acrobats and tumblers rather than dancers. Like the actors of Shakespeare's day such people were not considered respectable. However, dancers were now needed and the King, apart from encouraging his new school, gave special permission for some male courtiers to appear on stage without fear of being disgraced.

By 1681 there were four ballerinas in Paris, although they were not ballerinas as we know them. We do not know exactly how they danced, but it was probably little more than a very elegant walking and posing.

After all, before this time women had not jumped or performed any strenuous steps at all. Previously, if an effect of flight was needed, complicated machinery had been used to lift the dancer through the air.

The five positions of the feet had been established by this time. They had not been invented by any one person, but had developed from the elegant 'turned-out' walk of the courtier. It had also been realized that being able to move the leg forwards only was very limiting. Turning out the feet, which gives dancers their special duck-like walk, frees the leg to lift sideways and up in an arc.

By the early part of the eighteenth century important teachers were beginning to question old rules and habits. Ballet had been carefully nursed along by its royal patrons and helped to develop, but it was not allowed to break away from the court and its customs. Dancers had learned technique and ballet masters had new ideas, but they were expected to continue to provide entertainments in the old style.

The most influential of these teachers was Jean-Georges Noverre who worked for a long time in Stuttgart in Germany. In his important writings (*The Letters of Noverre*) he called for the abolition of masks to allow facial expression, the simplification of cumbersome court dresses which stopped the ballerina performing so many steps, and also for performances of dance alone, without the drama and song which had always accompanied it. Most important of all, he wrote that dance should be used to say something and not merely be decorative or just a trivial entertainment. His ideas would not be used fully until the end of the century, but during his lifetime great changes were made and two ballerinas in particular helped to make them.

Marie de Camargo was the most famous dancer of her day. She is said to have been the first ballerina to perform such steps as the *entrechat* which had previously only been performed by men. To do this she had to raise the hem of her dress a little; the first important step to freeing the ballerina from the hooped skirt. The other ballerina, Marie Sallé, went a step further, but had to leave Paris to do so. She wanted to dance her own ballet *Pygmalion* wearing only classical Greek draperies, but this caused a scandal at the Paris Opéra. She fled to London where the social attitude appeared less strict and had some success at Covent Garden in 1734. It would be many years before Paris would see such a sight!

Before the French Revolution changed the whole social scene in France, one other important event took place. In Bordeaux a pupil of Noverre, called Dauberval, had the idea for a ballet which he called *La Fille Mal Gardée*. It seemed to him to be the perfect story to show real people on the stage for the first time in a serious ballet. In different versions this ballet has been danced by companies around the world since its first performance in 1789.

The French Revolution not only swept away the French court, but also brushed aside many of the restrictions on ballet. By the beginning of the nineteenth century, there were many exciting ideas in the air and the Romantic era of the ballet was born.

This short period has left us two ballets which you can still see today. They are *La Sylphide*, the story of the young Scotsman and the Sylph, and *Giselle*. They have in common, a first act full of real people, farmers in Scotland and peasants in Germany, and a second act full of supernatural beings set in mysterious forests. From this time too we have the image of the ballerina I described at the beginning. In her long white skirt she has appeared in countless ballets since Marie Taglioni, the greatest ballerina of the age, first appeared on stage as a ghostly nun. Her frail, but very strong, physique and the impression of lightness she created, was something completely new. The newfound ability of the ballerina to stand on her toes, though she only wore soft shoes at this time, helped her achieve the impression of flight.

The public worshipped these ballerinas even more than fans adore

---

The playbill for the first production of *The Sleeping Beauty* in 1890.

СПЯЩАЯ КРАСАВИЦА.

Балетъ-феерія въ 3-хъ дѣйствіяхъ съ прологомъ.
Содержаніе заимствовано изъ сказокъ Перро, музыка П. И. Чайковскаго; постановка и танцы соч. балетмейстера М. Петипа.

ДЕКОРАЦІИ:

Прологъ — «Дворецъ Флорестана», Г-на Левотъ.
1-й актъ — «Дворцовый садъ», Академика Бочарова и Г-на Андреева.
2-й актъ — «Лѣсная мѣстность и панорама», Академика Бочарова.
«Внутренность дворца спящей красавицы», Г-на Иванова.
3-й актъ — «Эспланада дворца Флорестана» и апоѳеозъ Профессора Шишкова.
Машины Г-на Бергера.

Роль «Авроры» исполн. Г-жа БРІАНЦА

ДѢЙСТВУЮЩІЯ ЛИЦА:

Флорестанъ XIV, король . . . . . . Г-нъ Кшесинскій 1.
Королева. . . . . Г-жа Чекетти.
Принцесса Аврора, ихъ дочь . . . . Г-жа Бріанца.
Принцы: Шери . . . . Г-нъ Бекефи.
Принцы: Шарманъ . . . . Г-нъ Облаковъ.
Принцы: Фортюнэ. . . . . Г-нъ Карсавинъ.
Принцы: Флеръ-де-пуа. . . . . . . Г-нъ Гиллертъ.
Каталабютъ, оберъ церемоніймейстеръ короля Флорестана . . . . . . Г-нъ Стуколкинъ.
Принцъ Дезирэ. . . . . Г-нъ Гердтъ.
Лакей . . . . Г-нъ Орловъ.
Галифронъ, наставникъ Принца Дезирэ Г-нъ Лукьяновъ.
Феи: Сирени . . . . Г-жа Петипа.
Феи: Канареекъ . . . . Г-жа Іогансонъ.
Феи: Віолантъ . . . . Г-жа Жукова 1.
Феи: Крошка . . . . Г-жа Куличевская.
Феи: Кандидъ . . . . Г-жа Недремская.
Феи: Флёръ-де-фаринъ . . . . . . Г-жа Андерсонъ.
Карабоссъ, злая фея . . . . Г-нъ Чекетти.

Капельмейстеръ Г-нъ Дриго.

Above
Vaslav Nijinsky in his role of the Golden Slave in *Schéhérazade*.

Above right
Olga Preobrajenskaya, one of the great ballerinas of the Imperial Ballet of the Tsar in St Petersburg. You can see how the style has changed over the years. She became a famous teacher in Paris, and among her pupils were the celebrated 'baby ballerinas' of the 1930s, Baronova and Toumanova. She lived to be ninety-two, dying in 1962.

their pop idols today, so much so that the personality of the ballerina became more important than the ballet. This led to the decline of the Romantic era after only fifteen years and serious artists left Paris to work in other places. Some went to Italy to become important teachers producing dancers for the future and some, including Marius Petipa, went to Russia. The dancer and teacher Bournonville had already returned to Copenhagen after seeing the first Romantic ballet, *La Sylphide*, and there he produced his own version which is the one you are most likely to see today. He also started a whole new tradition of wonderful dancing which still continues in Denmark where his ballets have been carefully preserved.

Once in Russia Marius Petipa began to produce the great ballets which form the next stage in the development of ballet—the Classical age.

Petipa's *Swan Lake* and *The Sleeping Beauty* are still amongst the most often performed ballets. His dancers, often from Italy, had improved their technique enormously and it was to show off such steps as the *fouetté* that the skirt was shortened to become the classical *tutu*. The ballerina once again reigned supreme and the male dancer did little more than support her. The bounding leaps and fast turns which you will see the Prince perform in his solo in *The Sleeping Beauty* today are very recent additions and would not have been seen by the ballet's original audience—the Russian Tsar and his court in St Petersburg.

Noverre had started a revolution against the old court habits and the French Revolution made further change possible. However, by the end of the nineteenth century, Petipa too had become set in his ways and began to make each new ballet in the same old way. A new young dancer, Mikhail Fokine, fought against this and was fortunate to meet the like-minded Serge Diaghilev.

Together they took a troupe of Russian dancers, including Anna

Tamara Karsavina, who formed a great partnership with Nijinsky, later settled in London and gave companies very useful advice on revivals of the ballets she had made famous such as *Carnaval* and *Le Spectre de la Rose*.

Mikhail Baryshnikov dancing the role of the Prodigal Son in the ballet Balanchine created for the Diaghilev company.

Pavlova and Vaslav Nijinsky, to Paris where they had an enormous success. They returned there each year, creating wonderful new works, such as *The Firebird* and *Petrushka*, for each season.

Eventually the Russian Revolution of 1917 cut them off from their homeland. Pavlova had left to form her own company and Nijinsky was already becoming mentally ill. Diaghilev, who directed the company without being a dancer, choreographer or musician himself, continued to find new talent, but by the time of his death in 1929 the company was past its best.

Diaghilev's dancers and choreographers dispersed and took ballet to many countries. Serge Lifar stayed in Paris to give new life to the Paris Opéra, Ninette de Valois and Marie Rambert were already forming British ballet, and eventually George Balanchine went to work in America.

From this time ballet history really stops being history as many of those dancers and teachers are still working. Today they direct companies, create inventive ballets and pass on their experience to young dancers.

Ballet Today

Many of the big national ballet companies as well as some of the private companies can be traced back to the death of Diaghilev and the disbanding of his company in 1929.

Diaghilev had once been told by a fortune-teller that he would die by water and had since avoided long ocean crossings such as those taken by his company when it visited South America and the United States. The prophecy, however, came true when he died in Venice, with its

Patrice Bart dancing the role of Albrecht in Mary Skeaping's charming production of *Giselle* for London Festival Ballet.

hundreds of canals and wide open lagoon.

At the time his company was on holiday, following a London season—dancers, designers, musicians and choreographers were scattered across Europe and America. There was no real attempt to bring them together again as there was no natural leader. Instead they all found new homes in different places, working with new companies, founding their own groups, or opening ballet schools.

In France, which had been the company's home for many years, the company's last great male dancer, Serge Lifar, took over the direction of the Paris Opéra and stayed in charge there for many years. He gave new life to a company which had lost its former glory and restored the prestige of the school which produced new ballerinas, such as Yvette Chauviré, and choreographers, such as Roland Petit.

Roland Petit now has a thriving company of his own based in Marseilles and is still creating very funny and witty ballets, just as he did towards the end of the Second World War and immediately afterwards. His productions of both the *Nutcracker* and *Coppélia* are full of inventive ideas with lots of spirited dancing. He also creates ballets for the Paris Opéra, using fine dancers, such as Michaël Denard, Patrice Bart and Patrick Dupont, which the school still produces, as well as international stars like Mikhail Baryshnikov and Peter Schaufuss.

Opposite
Maurice Béjart was a French dancer, but his fame lies in Brussels where he founded his company, Ballet of the Twentieth Century. One of his large productions was a spectacle based on the life of Nijinsky in which Nijinsky (right) can be seen with dancers representing his great roles: the Faun, the Golden Slave, the Spirit of the Rose and Petrushka.

Above
Antoinette Sibley in *Cinderella* with the choreographer, Frederick Ashton, as one of the Ugly Sisters.

Long before the end of the Diaghilev company, some of its dancers had already begun the new ballet tradition. In Britain Anna Pavlova had formed a company made up of English girls, whom she found very well behaved and easy to control, to tour the world. It seems that their one-night stands and short seasons took them to almost every small city and town imaginable. They danced in Australia and Japan as well as North and South America. What they danced was often not of a very high standard, but Pavlova's own great artistry always made the ballets seem better. This little troupe prepared the ground for other companies to follow. It created a new audience who wanted to see more ballet and also influenced a whole generation of little girls who wanted to take up ballet as a career.

In Britain both Marie Rambert, a Polish dancer, and the Irish Ninette de Valois had started work. They had both danced with Diaghilev's company and Rambert had helped Nijinsky understand the very complicated rhythms of Stravinsky's music for *The Rite of Spring*. She opened her school and then a small theatre, the Mercury, in the last years of the First World War. If you ever see the film *The Red Shoes* you will see Moira Shearer dance the second act of *Swan Lake* on the tiny stage of the Mercury, watched by a small audience including, for one fleeting moment, Marie Rambert herself. Her special talent was to discover and encourage young choreographers. Over the next twenty years these would include Antony Tudor and Frederick Ashton who had been inspired to dance after seeing Anna Pavlova in Lima, Peru.

Ninette de Valois's talent was to have the vision to see how a national ballet could be formed and to have the drive and organizing ability to arrange it. The companies she formed at Sadler's Wells Theatre in London in the 'thirties were based on her school, but also used the talents discovered by Rambert. These companies went on to become the Royal Ballet of today. Soon after it was first formed, Frederick Ashton joined as resident choreographer and began to work with the very young Margot Fonteyn for whom he would create so many wonderful roles over the following thirty years.

Ninette de Valois was Director of the Royal Ballet until 1963 when she was followed first by Frederick Ashton, and then Kenneth MacMillan. The company is directed today by Norman Morrice, originally a member of the Ballet Rambert and yet another of Marie Rambert's discoveries.

Kenneth MacMillan was one of the young choreographers of the Royal Ballet to be discovered after the Second World War, along with John Cranko. At the same time Peter Darrell was creating his first ballets, before founding the Western Theatre Ballet which brought many new ideas to British ballet. From this company has grown the Northern

Ballet and the Scottish Ballet which he still directs. MacMillan still creates exciting ballets for the Royal Ballet, such as *Anastasia* and *Mayerling*. John Cranko produced very individual and often very funny ballets such as the much-loved *Pineapple Poll*, before he went on to found his great company in Stuttgart, Germany.

In the early years of British ballet two of Diaghilev's great stars, Alicia Markova and Anton Dolin, helped the young companies before they joined the newly formed American Ballet Theater. After the war, at the time of the Festival of Britain which was designed to cheer everyone up and show that the hard times of war were past, these two dancers founded their own company, London Festival Ballet. Now, over twenty-five years later, it is a major international company with important international dancers alongside its regular company members. The ballets they dance throughout Britain, as well as in Europe and America, include the Diaghilev treasures such as *Petrushka* which have been very carefully produced, as well as important new productions by Rudolf

The National Ballet of Canada dancing *Kettentanz* choreographed by Gerald Arpino, resident choreographer with the Joffrey Ballet.

Above
Lucette Aldous and Rudolf Nureyev in his production of *Don Quixote* for the Australian Ballet.

Opposite
John Cranko created many very funny ballets, including *Card Game* to Stravinsky's music. Other Cranko works which can be seen in many countries are *Pineapple Poll* and *Romeo and Juliet*.

Nureyev (*Romeo and Juliet* and *The Sleeping Beauty*) and Peter Schaufuss (*La Sylphide*). Although they no longer take a part in the direction of the company both Markova and Dolin are wonderful coaches for the younger dancers, helping them with roles they originally made famous.

With help and inspiration from the Royal Ballet and Ninette de Valois, ballet was encouraged in Australia and Canada. Some Russian dancers had stayed on in Australia following tours by different companies and out of the schools and groups they formed came the Australian Ballet, originally headed by Peggy van Praagh who had worked with the Sadler's Wells Ballet in London. She was soon joined by Robert Helpmann, who had played an important part in the growth of British ballet as Fonteyn's partner and as an inventive choreographer of ballets such as *Hamlet* and *Miracle in the Gorbals*.

Canada did not have such a strong background although the Royal

Winnipeg Ballet, made 'Royal' long before the British Royal Ballet, had been giving performances for many years. In the space of just twenty-five years the National Ballet of Canada has been formed with a large successful school. They often tour outside Canada and bring many ballets by Frederick Ashton to audiences in North America.

John Cranko gave Germany its first really important international company when he went to Stuttgart in 1960 to put on his ballet *The Prince of the Pagodas* for the company there. He found a wonderful ballerina, Marcia Haydée, for whom he would create many other great roles and in a very short time he built up a company with a 'family' feeling who worked together very well. It was not long before dancers he had trained went to other cities in Germany and revived the old opera house companies where nothing very important had ever happened. In particular John Neumeier has had success with his company in Hamburg. It too is like a family, as he works with the same few trusted friends time after time. His version of *The Nutcracker*, which takes a new look at this favourite old story, is the one you stand the best chance of seeing.

Although Denmark had both Fokine and Balanchine working there during the 1920s they gave most importance to the old ballets we have already talked about, ballets such as *La Sylphide* and *Napoli*. They also gave great importance to their school and, unlike most other companies in the world, always managed to produce a lot of good male dancers: something they still do. Dancers such as Peter Martins and Peter Schaufuss are amongst the most outstanding in the world today and they have been joined outside Denmark by others such as Adam Luders and Ib Andersen. One of the greatest dancers, Flemming Flindt, was Director until very recently and he introduced many unusual ballets into their programmes. Unfortunately, with the possible exception of *The Lesson*, a strange tale of a ballet teacher who kills his pupils, you are not likely to see many of them performed.

It is still the Bournonville ballets which bring fame to the company especially as they are becoming more common around the world in different versions. Only ten years ago there would have been little opportunity for you to see one; now there must be at least one production in the programmes of most companies, large and small. The Scottish Ballet have two full-evening ballets and companies such as the American Ballet Theater and the National Ballet of Canada dance *La Sylphide*. Even the New York City Ballet dances excerpts from *Napoli* and other ballets.

The Royal Ballet in Sweden had its greatest moments over two hundred years ago and, until recently, has not done anything of international importance. Now the company has very strong dancers and gives programmes which include the best ballets from several other countries. The school is becoming increasingly important and, like Denmark, is now producing many good boys, some of whom are already appearing with other companies.

Following the Revolution of 1917, ballet in Russia was cut off for many years. Immediately after the Revolution there were calls for the abolition of ballet altogether as it had been part of the hated court of the Tsar. Fortunately the official in charge of culture was not only a ballet lover, but also a friend of Lenin, so ballet was saved. Choreographers did, however, have to make ballets which kept to a safe party line. They had to be about the hard-working Soviet people and evil always had to be defeated. Even *Swan Lake* had to have a happy ending as it would have been unthinkable that evil could ever win! The first great Russian ballet of this period which you can still see was *Romeo and Juliet* in which Ulanova gave one of her greatest performances. This was filmed and is often shown. These big ballets, made to fit the monster stage of the Bolshoi Theatre, continued up to *Spartacus*, the story of the slaves' revolt against the power of Rome.

The main impact of Russian ballet has continued to be its brilliant dancers, whether they are from the athletic Bolshoi school with its big

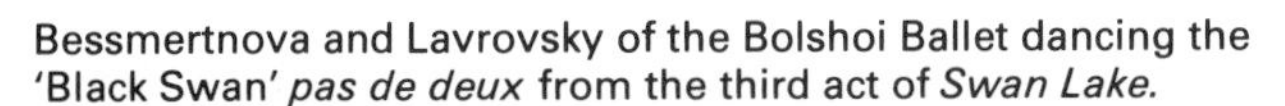

Bessmertnova and Lavrovsky of the Bolshoi Ballet dancing the 'Black Swan' *pas de deux* from the third act of *Swan Lake.*

jumps, or from the more refined and classical Kirov school of Leningrad. These dancers fit in more easily with the style of the West. You will remember that the dancers who left Russia with Diaghilev, to form the Western style, also came from Leningrad (then St Petersburg). The Kirov has unhappily lost some of its best dancers to the West, dancers such as Natalia Makarova, Rudolf Nureyev, Mikhail Baryshnikov and Galina and Valery Panov. Only recently have dancers come to the West from the Bolshoi Ballet of Moscow and their style is very different from that of the companies they now dance with. The Russian influence is seen across Eastern Europe where there are many companies, and on to Japan and Cuba.

In Cuba there is a major company, with a strong programme, led by Alicia Alonso who danced some of her greatest performances in ballets by Antony Tudor and others for the American Ballet Theater in the 1940s and '50s.

The story of American ballet in its present form starts with a stroke of luck for the United States. George Balanchine was not able to take up the position of ballet master at the Paris Opéra which was offered to him after the death of Diaghilev. Instead he worked in several places, including Copenhagen and London, settling nowhere. Then he accepted an invitation from Lincoln Kirstein to go to America and start a ballet school. Soon he was creating dances for the students of the School of American Ballet and some of them have become modern classics.

Like all small companies the early American ones got together, gave performances, disbanded through lack of money and formed again under new names. Balanchine created ballets for all these enterprises, as well as for the Ballets Russes companies which toured America.

These were the two companies which tried to take over the Diaghilev name. Their story is very, very complicated and a lot of their time seems to have been taken up with court cases and arguments. Both would claim to be the only people allowed to dance a particular ballet and both would argue about their titles! They did, however, do ballet a very good service by keeping public interest alive as well as providing work for many of the Diaghilev ballerinas. They also provided a base for Massine, who created some great works for them, including *Gaité Parisienne* and his symphonic ballets. These were important as, for the first time, a choreographer took a very famous piece of orchestral music like Tchaikovsky's *Pathétique* Symphony, and set dances to it. Some music critics were horrified by the whole idea. These companies were finally forced to stop touring and many of their dancers stayed in America to found schools in many towns and cities.

In 1948 the New York City Ballet was formed under the direction of Balanchine who heads it still. For the company he has created many

Gelsey Kirkland and Mikhail Baryshnikov in Jerome Robbins' *Other Dances*.

works in his special style of neo-classicism, which is discussed in the section on choreography. To dance these works he also developed, through the School of American Ballet, a particular type of ballerina which you will recognize immediately if you have ever seen ballerinas such as Suzanne Farrell or Gelsey Kirkland.

Balanchine was joined at the New York City Ballet by Jerome Robbins, the most brilliant young choreographer of the years after the Second World War. He had been brought up in the American Ballet Theater, a large company formed just before the war. Since then it has had big ups and downs, as it has had to depend a great deal on private money. It also plays very popular programmes which means that from time to time dancers are unhappy having no new roles to dance. Often its own dancers have been upset when, to bring in a big audience, they have had to depend on big guest stars such as Natalia Makarova and Mikhail Baryshnikov. They now have their own star, the brilliant young Cuban dancer Fernando Bujones.

Jerome Robbins made many clever ballets for the New York City Ballet including *The Concert*, one of the funniest ballets ever. For a time he had his own small company and he also worked on big Broadway shows such as *West Side Story* and *Fiddler on the Roof.*

Across America there are many other classical companies, often connected to universities. Unlike Britain, America can offer ballet students a course where ballet is one of the main subjects, and these students can work alongside professional dancers. Many eminent dancers have held posts as Professor of Dance in these universities, dancers such as Alicia Markova and Jacques d'Amboise.

In New York the main independent classical ballet company is the Joffrey Ballet which has an interesting list of ballets including works by Frederick Ashton and John Cranko, as well as classics from the Diaghilev company, alongside the regular creations of the resident choreographer, Gerald Arpino. The company has many financial problems and frequently does not dance for quite long periods which is a great pity as it has an important part to play in American ballet life.

America is the home of modern dance, a completely different dance form which began at the beginning of this century. In spite of this some of the most important experiments in mixing modern dance and classical ballet have taken place in Europe after years of the two dance forms keeping well out of each other's way.

Modern dance was started by people who thought that ballet was artificial, over-decorated and not connected with real life. Isadora Duncan started her work in the early years of this century in America, but made her biggest impact in Europe. She influenced Mikhail Fokine long before he left Russia and impressed the Revolutionary government of Russia so much that they invited her to form a company there. Isadora drew the most fantastic publicity and brought the new dance to everyone's notice. She wore flimsy dresses which allowed her body to move freely and danced in bare feet in order to feel the ground. Her idea was that the dancer should use the ground and not always try to jump and fly away from it, as in classical ballets. She chose subjects which she thought important at the time and created dances about revolution and freedom. Her style really only suited her and it would be left to other dancers to develop a real system of training.

In America Ruth St Denis and her husband Ted Shawn gave modern dance recitals and started the important Denishawn School, from which Martha Graham graduated. Although there were many other important people in these early years of modern dance it is Graham who has been the most influential. We are not going to talk about modern dance

---

Martha Graham's *The Owl and the Pussycat* with Tim Wengerd as the Owl and Liza Minnelli as the Narrator.

Dancers of the Nederlands Dans Theater in Nils Christe's *Miniatures*

technique here in detail, but it is interesting to see how many of Graham's students (and now even Graham herself, for she is still working, though in her eighties) have moved closer to the classical ballet. At first Martha Graham was completely against it. She says that she had to be in order to preserve her own ideas. Now that her form of dance is accepted, she feels that the two art forms can benefit from each other.

Nowadays you will find companies, such as the British Royal Ballet, dancing works by choreographers who would normally be labelled 'modern'. Hans van Manen from Holland has created a beautiful ballet for Anthony Dowell, one of the most classical male dancers. Glen Tetley, famous for his modern dances for the Ballet Rambert and the Nederlands Dans Theater, has created many works for the British Royal Ballet, London Festival Ballet and American Ballet Theater. Following the death of John Cranko, he even became director of the purely classical Stuttgart Ballet.

Modern dance companies and choreographers too have benefited from this more co-operative atmosphere. They now employ steps which before would have been found too 'classical'; steps such as little beats and jumps. These have helped to make the technique more light and airy, when before it was heavy and often gloomy. There is now a whole generation of choreographers who work with equal ease in both types of dance. Often they have received classical training, like Robert North of the London Contemporary Dance Theatre, while someone with modern training, like Nils Christe of the Nederlands Dans Theater, will bring a fresh eye to classical dancing.

Every art form has to develop. We must keep the classic ballets from each stage of the history of ballet to act as standards by which we can measure progress. Even these ballets undergo changes, as we have seen. Performances of *The Sleeping Beauty* today probably look very little like the original. If we were to try to keep things the same, ballet performances would be like visiting the most dusty and boring museum.

Ballet came from the social dances of the courts of the Renaissance and then caught the magic and mystery of the Romantic age. As people became interested in the customs of foreign lands, this brought their colourful dances to the stage. The classical ballet reflected the glory of the court of the Russian Tsar and the Diaghilev company brought life and vitality back to the West. Balanchine created an American way of dancing, just as Martha Graham did in a different field. It seems very natural that today ballet should be influenced by disco dancing.

What Makes a Ballet?

A ballet can be a sumptuous production taking a whole evening, involving dozens of dancers in elaborate costumes, monumental decor and a large-scale score needing a full symphony orchestra. Likewise, ballet can be one dancer, dressed in plain practice clothes, working in a tiny makeshift theatre with simple lighting and a pianist.

These would be two extremes and between them lie dozens of different types of ballets. In general they will be a mixture of choreography, dancing, designs and music. You cannot have a ballet without the first two items, although the last two can be left out. Even then you will be conscious of what the dancer is wearing. There may be no designer mentioned, but the picture you see of a dancer in street or practice clothes will create an impression. There may be no music, but the movements themselves will create a rhythm in your mind. It's not there, but it is understood.

The Choreography

The choreography is the creation and arrangement of the steps of the ballet. As you will see in the chapter about putting on a ballet, the choreographer is much more than just a creator of steps. In the ballet he or she is usually the person who has had the idea for the whole production. When the word is used in a musical production, or in a film, it means the more precise work of inventing steps inside a production devised by someone else. The writers of the musical will present the choreographer with a piece of music, a story, a setting and characters already created. Steps have then to be invented to suit the occasion.

The title of 'choreographer', meaning a composer of steps, rather like a composer of music, is a twentieth-century term. For many years choreography meant the writing down of steps. This is now referred to as dance notation in general and Labanotation or Choreology in particular. These are the two most commonly used systems, although there have been many others since the beginning of ballet.

Originally the creator of a spectacle, to be performed either in a courtyard or ballroom, would have been the dancing master. He would have been equally good at arranging steps and patterns for the courtiers or for their horses which were included in more spectacular efforts. He would travel about Europe collecting new ideas from others and spreading his own. He would probably not have been a dancer himself as the idea of the professional dancer had not yet established itself. He can be seen more as a producer of spectacles in which individual steps and the expressive use of the body of one person were not important. People would move together and it would be the complicated patterns they

Robert Helpmann, who played the Don, rehearsing Lucette Aldous in the Australian Ballet's *Don Quixote* when it was being filmed.

created which would give the effect. The only really individual expression would be left, for instance, to the grotesque characters who would decorate the large floats or chariots which would be drawn in during a banquet.

The dancing master gradually became a ballet master as the art of ballet took shape and the Academy formed by Louis XIV began to organize it seriously. Nowadays the ballet master is the person who teaches the class, arranges daily schedules and rehearses ballets created by other choreographers.

The ballet master remained the creator of the dances right up to the beginning of this century. Petipa, as ballet master, created the great classics without knowing he was a choreographer! Even in the Diaghilev company, which operated from 1909 to 1929, the resident choreographer was referred to as the ballet master. The person who held the post of *régisseur* was in charge of producing the ballets and organizing rehearsals. Gradually the word came into common usage. For instance during the growth of British ballet, Frederick Ashton worked purely as a choreographer and not as ballet master. Perhaps this had something to do with the way choreographers were gradually becoming independent from companies. There had been independent choreographers before, but most held resident posts with the state companies. Now the work was becoming split into the two jobs we know today.

In the section on the making of a ballet I go into detail about the day-to-day work of choreographers and how they approach different types of ballets. Here we can think about the different styles of choreography; the different styles by which we can describe the ballets.

Romantic ballets are those such as *La Sylphide* or *Giselle* and the other ballets created in that style long after. For instance *Les Sylphides* is a romantic ballet though it was created over sixty years after the end of the Romantic age. What makes a romantic ballet? First of all it should be made clear that the term does not refer to romance in the sense of love, although that plays a part in some of the stories. It is really the supernatural settings and characters which set the style and also the way they are danced—a soft style with very graceful arms and hands, often with broken (bent) wrists. The costumes of the ballerina, too, tell you that you are watching a romantic ballet—the long skirt of tulle, falling from the tight waist of a satin bodice with short sleeves just off the shoulders; the hair tightly drawn back into a bun. Taglioni was the first and perhaps most perfect romantic ballerina. In recent years the style was captured by the great Alicia Markova and is now being danced to perfection by ballerinas such as Eva Evdokimova and Natalia Makarova.

Narrative ballets tell a story. They can be created in any of the styles we will talk about here, whether romantic or classical or very, very modern, except of course the abstract style which means exactly the opposite as we shall see.

Demi-caractère ballets are those such as *Coppélia* or *La Fille mal Gardée.* They tell the story of ordinary people. The heroes and heroines are not gods and goddesses, sprites or wilis. They are farmers or peasant girls, village bumpkins or fiery Spanish gypsies. The settings are realistic. There are no haunted forests, just village squares or harvest fields. Even when you think there is a touch of magic, as in *Coppélia*, the dolls turn out to be just the clockwork inventions of an old man. Usually there are colourful escapades, misunderstandings and muddles as well as plenty of colourful dances. Mazurkas, czardas, tarantellas and waltzes fill the stage with swirling movements. And at the end the hero and heroine usually sort out their problems or escape from misadventure to live happily ever after—but not in a fairy-tale world; they will go back home to their farm, cottage or shop.

The very opposite of this type of ballet is the pure classical ballet, *The Sleeping Beauty* or *Swan Lake*. Here the style is very grand and the ballerina, around whom it revolves, is even grander. When these ballets were first made, she had just acquired the sort of technique you would expect today, although it is very interesting to read that the *prima ballerina assoluta* at the Maryinsky Theatre in St Petersburg, Mathilde Khessinskaya, was not a very good dancer, having rather unattractive legs and hardly ever going onto full point.

The form of these ballets followed the structure of the court. Just as there were different levels of civil servant and nobleman, leading up to the Tsar at the peak, so the ballet company would be graded from the lowliest *corps de ballet* member through the various degrees of soloist up to the ballerinas. Each one would expect to dance a piece made especially to fit her position and there would be trouble for the ballet master if this was not so. Petipa was excellent at coping with this and even added an extra solo in one of his ballets for Khessinskaya. She had not been included in the original cast, but, after her complaints to several grand dukes, Petipa was instructed to include her. She also wore all her own jewellery, real diamonds and pearls, on stage, which did not please the costume designers.

The classical ballets followed a fairly similar pattern, one you can see most clearly in *Swan Lake* and *The Sleeping Beauty*. Everything was designed as a frame for the ballerina, with her Prince firmly in the background.

Once the classical ballet had become such a formula that young choreographers began to rebel against it, notably Mikhail Fokine, creator of *Les Sylphides*, there were experiments with several types of ballets in the Diaghilev company.

Towards the end of its life George Balanchine created the first ballet in the neo-classical style, *Apollo*. You will hear this description applied to many works now made by choreographers ranging from Frederick Ashton to John Neumeier. Of course they do not work exclusively in this style, which is still seen in its purest form in Balanchine's works for the New York City Ballet.

Balanchine had been a student at the Imperial School and knew the

The choreographer tries it out and then the dancers copy: Sally Owen and Nelson Fernandez of Ballet Rambert work with Norman Morrice who is now the Director of the British Royal Ballet.

ballets of Petipa at first hand. He took the pure dance part of these ballets and discarded all the unnecessary trappings. Working with the strict classical steps, those you will see Aurora make in *The Sleeping Beauty* or the grand ones from *The Nutcracker pas de deux*, Balanchine told the story of the growth of Apollo and the inspiration of the muses of music, mime and drama. From this he has developed the clean, pure style associated with the New York City Ballet today.

Abstract ballets are those which do not have a story. They may have a slight theme, but usually that theme is taken from the mood of the music. Here bodies move to music, creating an impression on eye and mind which you should not be able to explain in a definite way. You might feel a mood of sadness, or it might leave you feeling very happy, but not by involving you in a sad story or a happy one.

You will often hear ballets referred to as 'modern ballets'. This term is difficult to explain as it does not mean anything precisely. It is also often confused with modern dance. Actually modern ballet means nothing more than ballets created today and either reflecting modern subjects or being purely abstract. Modern ballet has to belong to today and today's modern ballets will not be tomorrow's. On the other hand Modern Dance refers to a school of dance, just as Classical Dance does. Modern Dance was Modern Dance when Isadora or Martha Graham first danced it and has remained so.

Modern ballets will usually be in a neoclassical style. That is, they can be danced in point shoes and will use recognizable ballet steps, perhaps changed in clever ways invented by the choreographer.

As you will remember from the history of ballet, all the different styles of choreography have come together, so that it is no longer easy to divide ballets up into types. This will give future choreographers greater scope. They will be able to explore many more interesting ideas than would ever be possible if they were confined to one style.

'. . . let's see now . . . do it like this . . .'—Lindsay Kemp, creator of such spectacles as *Cruel Garden* for Ballet Rambert, working with Lucy Burge.

The Dancing

Choreography has developed alongside improvements in dancing technique. From the beginning of dance the ability of the dancer to perform certain steps has given the choreographer more ways of expressing his feelings or telling his story. The development of both is so interconnected that it is sometimes impossible to say which came first. Perhaps a dancer working alone might find that he or she could add to a step already known. Perhaps a choreographer would ask the dancer to try a new way of movement and out of this a standard step would develop.

The great Russian ballerina, Galina Ulanova, sits with her pupil Ekaterina Maximova during a break in rehearsals at the Bolshoi Theatre. Ulanova created the role of Juliet in the famous Russian production of *Romeo and Juliet* which was made into a film.

It is very difficult to put exact dates on particular steps. We can only show a general period during which the step developed. Turn-out, in which the feet form a straight line from toe to heel and heel to toe, developed over the seventeenth century and was credited to the ballet master Pierre Beauchamps. However, he did not invent the position, he just arranged into a set form what was then a common practice. By the beginning of the eighteenth century men could perform jumps, but ballerinas, still wearing their hooped skirts, could not. Pirouettes, or turning movements, were similarly impossible. Marie Camargo introduced the *entrechat* and by the middle of the century the German ballerina Anne Heinel performed the first *pirouette à la seconde*, in which the dancer turns with one leg held out to the side.

As costume became freer so the ballerina was able to extend her technique until it reached a point during the Romantic age when she completely took over the ballet from the male dancer. By then she could also stand on point, if only for brief moments.

Later in the nineteenth century, ballerinas trained in Italy made their appearances in Russia and caused a sensation with the steps they could perform. For instance Pierina Legnani could perform *fouettés* which she was not taught by Petipa. He was simply clever enough to use her ability in the drama of the third act of his *Swan Lake*.

All the more exciting steps we now know are based on the old teachings. Only the more athletic jumps, often devised in Russia, are new. It is simply the technical ability of dancers today which make the steps look more exciting. Dancers now jump higher, turn faster and balance longer than their predecessors. A greater part of the fame and appeal of ballerinas such as Pavlova and Karsavina, lay more in their power of interpretation than in the steps they could perform. Of course we must remember that in those days audiences had nothing to compare them to. The colour of Russian ballets and the temperament of the dancers were all new. They also could see far fewer performances. Dancers nowadays have to improve constantly because we see them so often. Dancers in the West, particularly the men, had to improve their techniques rapidly when Rudolf Nureyev defected from Russia.

Technique is constantly improving. Only ten years ago the male dancer could quite happily make a very simple variation in one of the classic *pas de deux*. Now, to make an impact, he absolutely has to do some really splendid turns and tricks. The art of the great dancer is to make the tricks look part of the performance and not a circus show.

But technique is not everything. It has to be used for some purpose. An evening of dancers trying to outdo each other with turns and jumps, as you might have seen at a gala for instance, can be very boring. The technique is there to give the choreographer freedom to create. If he knows that the dancer has a great range he will feel free to try out new ways of showing character or story. Some of the contortions in a *pas de deux* by Kenneth MacMillan, for instance (and he is perhaps one of the greatest living creators of them), look smooth and easy when you see them. You are not immediately aware of ballet steps individually, for the

Opposite
Rudolf Nureyev as a young student at the famous Kirov School in Leningrad.

Above
Nadezhda Pavlova, the brightest young star of the Bolshoi Ballet. She comes from one of the Russian regional companies, Perm, which now send many talented dancers to the big companies.

technique of dancers like Lynn Seymour is blended in with natural movements.

As both of the dancers who talk in this book tell you, today they must not just dance and be manipulated like puppets by the choreographer. They also give a lot themselves. Not only are steps put into ballets by the dancers themselves, under the guidance of the choreographer, but important parts of characters too. Kenneth MacMillan can ask Lynn Seymour to express a particular emotion in her own way. She does so and he then polishes it into the shape he wants. In a sense this means that dancers today have to be more intelligent. They must read books for background information; they must understand difficult music, much more difficult than the rhythms of Stravinsky which Nijinsky had to cope with.

The dancer starts every day with a class of about an hour and a half.

This class is still much the same as the ones given at the beginning of the last century. After class there will be a rehearsal of old roles or new ballets and the day may end with a performance. It is now one of the most tiring jobs there is, mentally and physically. Not for nothing are dancers called the work-horses of the theatre!

The Music

In the early years of the dance, when it was not ballet as we know it, the travelling dancing masters, who arranged the spectacles, were also talented musicians and instrumentalists. They were often violinists and, up to the beginning of this century, the violin, not the piano, was used to accompany the ballet class. If you have a chance to see the Bournonville ballet *Conservatoire* or study the ballet paintings by Degas you will notice that the ballet master carries a small violin.

One of the most important composers in these early years was the Italian, Lully, who worked mostly in France at the court of Louis XIV. He was court violinist and director of music and a great supporter of the dance. He had been a very talented dancer in his youth and included lively dances in his productions, some of which were arranged by the great dramatist Molière. Incidentally, he conducted by beating the floor with a stick, which must have rather interfered with the music, and during one performance he hit his foot. The bruise did not heal and he died from blood poisoning.

During the eighteenth century, when Noverre was putting forward his ideas about *ballet d'action* (the earliest 'story' ballets), Mozart wrote his only ballet, *Les Petits Riens*. Before this Gluck had written an important score, for *Don Juan*, but, generally, the nearest composers got to writing music which helped the action along was something like the music which accompanied silent films. It was music to accompany pantomime and in one composition there was even a piece called 'hurry music'. You can imagine what it must have sounded like.

In the nineteenth century, with the arrival of the Romantic age, one of the most important pieces of music written especially for dance made its first appearance. This was the score for the Danish version of *La Sylphide*. Bournonville could not use the original Paris score (it was too expensive) so he asked the young Danish Baron Hermann von Løvenskjold to write a new one. You can find out more about this in the section dealing with the most recent production of this lovely ballet.

Giselle by Adolphe Adam had several of the same ideas, particularly the use of a theme tune for the different characters. This score has often

Edgar Degas' painting *'Le Foyer de la Danse'*.

been dismissed as uninteresting, but it is full of wonderful ideas and suits the story perfectly.

After *Giselle*, which was changed many times and nowadays often includes the 'Peasant' *pas de deux* written by Burgmüller, there was a break of thirty years before the next piece of important ballet music. That was *Coppélia* by Leo Delibes who also composed *Sylvia* which you stand less chance of seeing (except in France), but which is just as full of good music.

Coppélia is one of the most beautiful ballet scores and is an important piece of music as well as a lively background for dancing. At this time in Russia, for instance, the long period when much of the ballet music would be written by the resident composer or conductor at the Imperial Theatre was just starting. It would be written to order and most of it would sound that way, though some of it is now considered more important than we have thought so far. You will know some of the melodies quite well, tunes for dances such as the *Don Quixote pas de deux*. The two main composers were Minkus and Drigo and their music had so many similarities that sometimes even ballet critics cannot distinguish

Opposite
Natalia Makarova dancing the spectacular *pas de deux* from *Don Quixote* with its exciting music by Minkus, who was resident composer to the Imperial Theatres of the Tsar.

Above
Suzanne Farrell and Peter Martins, the leading dancers of the New York City Ballet, in the 'Diamonds' section of George Balanchine's *Jewels* danced to Tchaikovsky's Third Symphony. The 'Emeralds' section is danced to music by Fauré and the 'Rubies' section to Stravinsky's *Capriccio for Piano and Orchestra*.

and identify new pieces. Any piece in doubt is referred to as being by Drinkus!

Coppélia was written just a few years before the first of Tchaikovsky's great scores, *Swan Lake*, which was a flop when first heard. He persevered and went on to write *The Sleeping Beauty*, which he liked best, and then *The Nutcracker*. This gave him difficulty at first as he did not think the story was grand enough.

I write elsewhere about the way Tchaikovsky worked and I am still amazed that he could produce these wonderful works to very precise instructions, bar by bar, from Petipa. Indeed he said that if he had had such guidance years before, *Swan Lake* would have been a success.

The one name you can never avoid at this point in the history of ballet is Diaghilev. He was responsible for bringing Igor Stravinsky into the ballet world. He heard a few pieces by the young composer at a concert and invited him to orchestrate, not compose, some pieces for the first Paris season of his ballet group in 1909. Later he asked him to write the music for *The Firebird* after his first choice had wasted many months. Stravinsky delivered the magnificent score exactly on time and the final grand scene of the coronation was his idea. Originally there were going to be wedding *divertissements*, which is surprising when you think that Fokine hated this sort of thing in other ballets.

Stravinsky became the single most important composer for the ballet in this century. He worked throughout the life of the Diaghilev company, very often in close co-operation with George Balanchine, a partnership which continued almost fifty years until Stravinsky's death.

The Diaghilev company used other great composers of the time, in particular Ravel (*Daphnis and Chloe*), Debussy (*Afternoon of a Faun*), Richard Strauss (*The Legend of Joseph*, which has been filmed recently for television, using the original music and John Neumeier's new choreography), and the French composers known as *Les Six*. They included Satie whose music Frederick Ashton used for *Monotones*, and Milhaud who wrote *The Creation of the World* using the fashionable black jazz rhythms of the time.

Diaghilev commissioned scores from these composers. Sometimes they went away and wrote the piece *they* wanted; at other times they worked very closely with the choreographer, something essential in the writing of a story ballet.

A commission like this can present great difficulties to the composer, but as you can see from the example of Tchaikovsky in the classical period, this need not stop them producing great music. In our time the American composer Aaron Copland has written some of his greatest music, such as *Appalachian Spring* for Martha Graham, to a very precise scenario.

Full-evening ballets, with specially written music, are not found very often for many reasons, often financial or practical, and it is clearly easier for a choreographer to use existing music.

Recent ballets which have special scores include George Balanchine's *Don Quixote*, which is by Nicholas Naboukov, so do not expect the rumpity-tump tunes which go with the *Don Quixote pas de deux* you are most likely to see. Most of the others tend to be for modern ballets such as *The Tempest* by Arne Nordheim, which Glen Tetley created for Ballet Rambert.

The most popular way of approaching a full-evening ballet is to rearrange existing pieces of music. Perhaps the most famous and most popular example of this is the score for *La Fille Mal Gardée* which John Lanchberry brought to life for Frederick Ashton. He used themes from all the previous productions and orchestrated them in his own lively style. Similar treatment by a variety of clever arrangers has been given to the music of Scarlatti (for Cranko's *The Taming of the Shrew*),

There have been many attempts to choreograph to the great symphonies, but perhaps one of the most controversial was Maurice Béjart's version of Beethoven's Choral Symphony, shown below.

Tchaikovsky (Cranko's *Onegin*, which uses lesser-known tunes and not the music from the opera *Eugene Onegin*) and Massenet (MacMillan's *Manon*, which again avoids the music for the opera of the same name).

Composing for an abstract ballet, which would usually be a one-act work, presents different problems. The choreographer has to convey the correct mood, the sense and tempo of the piece. Having done this the composer goes away and writes and hopefully produces something which fulfils the choreographer's wishes. As you can imagine this is a risky business as any composers of note must be allowed freedom to express themselves, but that freedom is necessarily limited by the picture the choreographer has of the ballet. Of course this is not such a major problem as I make it seem as most choreographers will naturally be drawn towards composers they admire and feel themselves in sympathy with.

By music we usually think of orchestral works or at least pieces for solo instruments or small groups. But if you see companies such as Maurice Béjart's Ballet of the Twentieth Century you will know that there are many other possibilities, the most important being electronic music, either alone or, in the case of Béjart, added to existing music. I can remember audiences in Germany being furious at the electronic gurgling sounds he added to the music for the Venice scenes of *The Tales of Hoffmann*.

Purely electronic music is finding its way very quickly into the repertoires of many classical companies and you are quite likely to see a ballerina on point dancing to the rhythmic beats of a moog synthesizer, an instrument you are sure to know if you follow any pop groups. Things are even going full circle and now orchestral composers write pieces for orchestras and singers in which they attempt to recreate the electronic sounds, as in Glen Tetley's *Greening* written by Arne Nordheim, or the works of the Polish composer Lutoslawski. Musicians hit, scratch and scrape their instruments, in fact they do everything except play them in the conventional way.

Then there are ballets in silence, the most famous being Jerome Robbins' *Movements*. Since Diaghilev's days there have been many experiments in this area, but few of them remain in the repertoire. I have seen companies rehearsing these ballets and it seems more like an arithmetic class. Dancers count the beats to themselves, as they do in classical ballets for instance, but this goes way beyond simple 1–2–3–1–2–3

Arlette van Boven and Hans Knill in Hans van Manen's *Solo for Voice 1*. The singer in the background makes some very unusual noises, exactly as written by the American composer John Cage, as she directs the two dancers around the stage.

rhythms. Counting over thirty in one sequence is the highest I ever heard. As you can see there is still music here, even if it is not played. The dancers move in rhythm and you create the music in your head. Only very advanced choreographers, like Merce Cunningham, really produce works without music, although at times music is playing! His whole world is something very exciting and very special, but not within the scope of this book. He is someone who has to be experienced and not written about. If his company appears near you I would recommend that you see them, but do not expect anything you have ever seen before!

Just as Cunningham is making his own rules, so every choreographer has his own way of working with the music. Some follow the beats, some put a step on every beat. Some use it as a mood background and others allow it to take over the drama. Their reaction is completely personal, depending on whether they are illustrating the music, using a tone poem, or letting music underline the story they are trying to tell.

Ballet and music, of one form or another, are so linked that it is hard to see them separated. In fact, just as different types of dance are now coming together, so composers and choreographers are collaborating to produce many wonderful new ideas.

The Designs

The designer plays a very important part in the success of a ballet. He or she provides much more than a pleasant background for the dancers, and will create the whole mood of the ballet, whether it is a classic requiring realistic settings or a modern ballet with abstract designs.

The earliest dances at court used designs by famous painters and architects as there were few artists who specialized in theatre design. In Italy, the Bibiena family created imaginative settings which used clever perspectives, while in England Inigo Jones, a great architect, designed settings for masques by Ben Jonson.

These designs were often only additions and decorations to the architecture of the court ballroom or the palace gardens, but gradually they developed into complete designs of the type you would expect to see today. Many were incredibly elaborate and very realistic. Machinery would often be included so that gods could vanish into the heavens, or devils into the earth, and the elaborate chariots, which carried entertainers into the great banquets, would be gilded and covered with expensive ornaments. They would be drawn by horses, elephants or camels, depending on the theme of the banquet.

The costumes for the court dancers would be modelled on court dress with additional jewellery and decoration. Only the common entertainers

Goncharova's décor for the last scene of *The Firebird* suggests a great Russian city of crimson and purple rising high above the stage where the splendid coronation ceremony of Ivan and the Princess takes place.

on the floats and chariots would wear anything theatrical or revealing. Dancers, like actors in Shakespeare's day, were not considered really respectable, so they were allowed to dress as satyrs and sprites, nymphs and mermaids. Ladies of the court would never have worn such costumes. If they represented a bird, for instance, the designer would create a fantastic headdress and mask out of exotic feathers, rather like you would wear for a fancy-dress party today, but the costume, though elaborate and colourful, would be modest.

When dance moved into the theatre and was performed completely behind a proscenium arch, the designer was presented with new problems. Before now, there had been arches in outdoor performances, but again like the drama, the audience were often placed all round the action and not directly in front of it. Before, the dancing area had always been clear, as the space covered was usually very large. Now the designer had to provide elaborate settings, but still leave ample space for the dancers to move.

By the Romantic age, beautiful atmospheric settings were being painted on back-cloths and drops and the effect of these was helped by the invention of gas lighting. The flickering lights were perfectly suited to the haunted glades and underwater scenes. Additional lighting came from the roof, which often had windows, and it was a long time before the lighting in the auditorium was put out during the performance.

Following this period when the different elements of design, costume, setting and lighting worked well together, things deteriorated, just as the ballet did itself. In Paris where the ballet became a social entertainment, the sets became more elaborate whether they were right for the ballet or not, and the audiences definitely preferred revealing costumes.

In Russia things were a little better as court etiquette still had to be followed, and it was here that a very important step in theatre design took place. Vsevolozhsky, the Director of the Imperial Theatres, was a talented artist and he envisaged a production where the costumes and designs blended perfectly with the production. That production was *The Sleeping Beauty*.

At roughly the same time the next major step took place when Diaghilev and his young collaborators, who were mostly artists, began the move to use the work of easel painters, instead of the resident designers of the state theatre, in designing ballets.

From these early thoughts Diaghilev developed the policy which he carried out with his own company, inviting the great painters of the day to design costumes. Picasso designed Massine's ballet *Tricorne*, Bakst designed *Schéhérazade* and Benois designed *Petrushka* in the early years. All these ballets, with carefully reproduced decor, can still be seen today. In the 1920s Marie Laurencin designed the beautifully chic setting for *Les Biches* and Marc Chagall designed Balanchine's *The Prodigal Son*. Both of these are still performed, the first by the British Royal Ballet and other companies, the second by the New York City Ballet as well as the British Royal Ballet.

During the same period, much more experimental work took place, including ballets with décor cut out of great sheets of perspex through which different lights were shone, an idea used up to this day in shows ranging from ballet to rock concerts.

Lighting has played an increasingly important part in stage design. It has several great advantages as it is relatively cheap compared to building sets and making costumes, and it presents few transport problems. Skilful lighting can create the most magical effects and interesting moods. It also leaves the stage space completely free for dancing.

Practical considerations such as this must always be in the designer's mind. Story ballets are particularly difficult, as they usually need realistic castles, thrones, houses or staircases. All of these have to be designed in such a way as to be convincing, but at the same time they must not get in the way of the dancers.

Abstract ballets are easier from a practical point of view, but have problems of their own. As there is no strong story the designer has to

The simple beauty of Sophie Fedorovich's décor for Frederick Ashton's classic work, *Symphonic Variations*, is hard to capture in a photograph. Its clean arcs and cool green shades create a marvellous architecture behind the dancers. In the bottom right-hand corner you can see Brian Shaw, one of the original cast in 1946, who is now principal teacher of the Royal Ballet.

work particularly closely with the choreographer if the set and costumes are going to reflect the latter's ideas properly. It would be useless if the choreographer was trying to create one mood and the designer quite separately produced costumes which suggested another. Nowadays you will see many abstract ballets and modern dances danced only in tights or variations of practice clothes, including knitted leg-warmers. Even these have to be designed, as the designer must know in advance how the lighting will affect the colours. Stage lighting has a different quality to ordinary light and can play many tricks with various fabrics by reflecting the light so that their actual colour or texture looks quite different when seen by the audience.

The designer has to oversee the make-up that the dancer will wear. He or she may want a particular exotic effect, such as the pale make-up devised by Nicholas Georgiadis for the last scene of Rudolf Nureyev's *The Sleeping Beauty*. Perhaps only a natural look is wanted, but even that has to be carefully worked out. In general, lighting today is so sophisti-

The American producer and choreographer, Alwin Nikolais, is also the master of stage tricks and wonderful lighting effects. In ballets such as *Tent* the dancers' bodies blend with the chiffon folds and mysterious lighting.

cated that dancers need wear very little make-up, not the layers of bases and lines which used to be necessary.

To top everything off, the designer will also create hair styles which can be anything ranging from a feather-decorated wig of falling curls for the last scene of *The Sleeping Beauty*, to a small decoration to lighten the severe romantic hairstyle in the second act of *Giselle*. There is much the same problem in designing an exotic style for a modern ballet, for example, the piled-up curls the girls wear in Hans van Manen's *Grosse Fuge*.

Having created the right ideas on paper the designer must next oversee each detail of creation in the workshop.

Producing a Ballet

When a ballet company announces a new work, an addition to its repertoire, this usually means one of three things. They may be preparing their own version of one of the classic ballets, perhaps *Swan Lake* or *La Sylphide*, or perhaps they will be starting upon a completely new project by one of their own members or a guest choreographer from some other company. The third possibility is that they will be reviving, in as near as possible its original form, a work from the past or one already being danced by another company.

Reviving the Past

If a company decide to revive a ballet, the problems are much simpler than either of the first two possibilities. If it is an old ballet, perhaps one originally made for the Diaghilev company, like *Schéhérazade*, or even one created much later, such as *Gaité Parisienne*, there is a very good chance that there are people still alive who remember the original production and can help with the choreography.

Many of the early ballets were not written down in dance notation when they were first made, but fortunately, over the last few years, very accurate records of them have been made. Perhaps because of the very healthy life they must lead, many ballet personalities live to a fine old age so that we have been able to benefit from their experiences. For instance Massine, who worked with Diaghilev from 1913, died only in 1979. Not only are we still able to use films of his ballets which he made many years ago, but he was able to supervise all the recent revivals and make sure that the versions written down for the future are accurate. It also means that there are now three generations of people active in the ballet who were able to work with him and capture his special style, something not easy to write down.

Of course, if it is an old ballet from the beginning of this century which is being revived, it is not necessary to be completely accurate in reproducing it, although the original designs will probably still exist and in many cases actual scenery has survived. However, since those days stage lighting has changed completely, not only with the introduction of electricity, but by more sophisticated ways of placing the actual lamps. Footlights, for which the original décor had to be much brighter and cruder than we now need, have long since become a thing of the past.

Below
Per-Arthur Segerström of the Royal Swedish Ballet as the Baron in their revival of Massine's *Gaité Parisienne*.

This has caused make-up to be adapted as well. No longer does the dancer wear many thick layers of different tones with every line carefully drawn in; a soft base with light tones and some soft eye shadows will be quite enough. Modern lighting will make sure that facial expressions are clear right up into the highest seats of the gallery.

Over the last fifty or sixty years another major change has been seen in the development of the dancer's technique. Originally Massine, or some other choreographer, would have had to work with male dancers who were still a product of the training of the Russian Imperial schools where, until the beginning of this century, they could look forward to spending a great deal of their time supporting a ballerina—not for nothing were they called *porteurs*. They would not be able to perform the spectacular steps male dancers execute today. As a result, when producing a modern version of one of these old ballets, it is quite fair to make the steps for the male dancer more interesting, both for him and for the audience, as long as they do not spoil the style of the ballet as a whole.

Some of these same problems arise when reviving even more recent ballets. Some choreographers, such as Maurice Béjart in Belgium and George Balanchine in New York, are not really interested in their ballets once they have been created. Of course they do supervise rehearsals as they want the performance to look its best, but their minds are usually on the next project, their next creation.

Today a dance notator will sit in at all rehearsals and by the time the ballet is presented on stage, a complete record, looking something like a music score, but with different symbols, will exist. Not so long ago, however, a work would be created, danced a few times during one season and, perhaps for some quite practical reason, not danced again for some time. Only five years later someone might suggest it should be danced again and what happens? The dancers, and quite often the choreographer as well, have forgotten the steps. This can mean approaching the new production like a jigsaw puzzle. All the people originally involved will be brought together in the hope that one dancer will remember one section while another will remember something else. I have found that quite often a dancer will forget what he or she was dancing, but remember someone else's part quite well, having watched them rehearsing so often, or just from being on stage at the same time.

As you can see, reviving a ballet is really a problem of catching the

---

On previous page
Frederick Ashton and his designer, Julia Trevelyan Oman, created a brief story to bring alive the friends of Edward Elgar whom he had pictured in his *Enigma Variations*.

right style. Something did once exist, however faint in people's memories, and it is up to the producer and dancers to recreate this to the best of their ability. Producing an original work, however, has completely different problems.

New Creations

How a new ballet is created is the most difficult process to describe. There are as many ways of doing it as there are choreographers. To take one choreographer as an example would be very misleading, as even one person will probably have several different ways of approaching different work.

The reasons why a choreographer does a particular work are just as varied, apart from the fact that like everyone else, they are all working professional people earning a living. The resident choreographer with a company will be expected, as part of his or her contract, to produce a ballet each season. This is following in the grand tradition of the great Petipa whose contract with the Imperial Theatre in St Petersburg laid down that he must create one major work each season. Among his grand total of over fifty ballets, he created *Don Quixote, La Bayadère, The Sleeping Beauty, The Nutcracker, Swan Lake* and *Raymonda*, not to mention producing the dances in over thirty operas.

The starting point of the ballet can be the music, which might suddenly appeal to a choreographer, or a story for which he or she will then either find existing music or ask a composer to write a new piece. Great music has indeed been written to order, from Tchaikovsky's ballets to Aaron Copland's *Appalachian Spring* written for Martha Graham.

When the decision has been made about the music, the choreographer is ready to start work. Whether it is to be pure dance or a story ballet, that first rehearsal, when the company wait for the choreographer to instruct them, can be very nerve-racking. If there is a story, it is easier to give the dancers some idea of what they are about to start on. If it is a pure dance work obviously it will not be easy to put into words so the dancers simply wait for the choreographer to set them in motion.

Some choreographers will start from a pattern and then closely follow the music. You will notice this in many of the ballets by the Dutch choreographer Hans van Manen. Some will work out steps by themselves and then ask the dancers to follow. As Lynn Seymour explains in her interview (page 85), Kenneth MacMillan will listen to the music and then try out very general movements, a run here, a pose there, following the sense of the music before turning these notions into recognizable ballet steps. His special talent is for double work, the *pas de deux*, and he

Alexandra Radius and Han Ebbelaar of the Dutch National Ballet in Hans van Manen's *Twilight*.

can devise wonderful ways of entwining a pair of bodies by working with the dancers in a studio.

In this type of ballet the dancer contributes very much more than in the classics or revivals of recent works. There they must supply good technique and deep characterization, but in the creation of new works they are asked to give more. A choreographer may ask the dancer to pose in a certain way and then rush across the room to a certain piece of music, without telling him exactly how. It may prove no use at all, or it may be kept in the ballet in exactly that way. A choreographer may ask a boy to lift a girl, which might prove impossible and they may fall. That too may find its way into the finished work. In *Serenade*, George Balanchine kept in such an accident, and also made a dramatic moment out of one girl arriving late.

As you can see, deciding upon a new work is a very risky business for a ballet company. They do not know what they have paid for until it is too late! Although they will have selected the choreographer after seeing some of his or her other works, they do often commission works from inexperienced young choreographers. This presents the Artistic Director of a company with a difficult decision, but it is one that has to be taken for the future good of ballet as a whole.

Renewing a Classic

Producing a new version of an established classic ballet combines all the problems we have come across so far. Briefly these are the problems of keeping the right style and being faithful to the original, while at the same time making it acceptable to a modern audience and creating new choreography to replace sections which have been lost or long since forgotten.

To give you some idea of what goes into the production I will take you step by step through the creation of one recent big production; *La Sylphide*, produced by Peter Schaufuss for the London Festival Ballet.

A company such as the London Festival Ballet has important London seasons, long tours around Britain and major visits overseas. In recent years they have danced in America and China. This means that they have to produce at least one full-length ballet each year as well as some short ones. They also give 'workshop' performances for young choreographers to try out their ideas.

The choice of a new work will have to take many things into account. It should suit the image of the company, it should be a work of some importance and it should fit into their programmes alongside other ballets. It also must have some chance of being popular with the public who will pay to see it. In these early days, as soon as the decision has been made to put on a new production, the next consideration is money.

The financing of a new production may not seem to have much to do with ballet as an art, but unless the company make careful plans about the way a production is going to pay for itself over the years, no ballet would ever reach the stage. It would be completely foolish for a company to decide to do a lavish production, regardless of cost. Some have, and the result is that those companies are no longer with us.

Where does the money come from? The most obvious source is you, the paying public, when you pay for your ticket along with millions of other people. If things worked perfectly, all that money would add up to pay the rent of the theatre, the salaries of the musicians, dancers, designers and choreographers, and the cost of making the costumes and scenery. Unfortunately it doesn't and never has.

Sometimes you may read about subsidies for the ballet and opera; money given by the national government, town authorities, or private individuals who do not expect either to make a profit or get any of it back at all. You may have seen headlines or letters of complaint asking why taxes should go up to pay for new ballets, or the even more expensive operas.

The answer is that these arts never have paid for themselves and the few companies who have made great efforts to perform in a commercial way, that is to balance their expenditure with the money received from the public, have never lasted very long.

Ballet has always been subsidized in one way or another. Private people in Paris in the nineteenth century were more than happy to pay very high prices to see pretty ballerinas (at that time it was the only chance of seeing a lady in public wearing very little clothing!) and to be able to go backstage to meet them. The Imperial Ballet in St Petersburg was part of the court of the Russian Tsar and was paid for out of Imperial funds. Very few tickets were sold to ordinary people for ballets such as *The Sleeping Beauty* or *Swan Lake* when they were first performed. Even the great Diaghilev, who managed to keep a large company together for twenty years, had to rely on wealthy art lovers who gave him generous gifts.

Now kings and queens cannot afford to keep large companies and wealthy individuals are fewer. The place of royal patronage has been taken by the state. In Britain the Arts Council is given money by the government to spend in the way it thinks best. In America the National Arts Endowment Fund plays much the same role. Some town and city authorities in Britain, especially London, support the ballet, but not on the scale you will find in Germany where many towns have a small ballet company. There are now well over sixty of these.

In America an important source of income is the big charitable institutions, such as the Ford Foundation. These give money without any artistic restrictions, but as an encouragement not to get too lazy they insist that for every dollar they give the company must find another dollar through its own efforts. As a result, companies such as the New York City Ballet have a wonderful array of items for sale, ranging from tee-shirts to bath towels. Don't expect a free pair of souvenir shoes from your favourite ballerina there; they are sold to help the company! There is a growing amount of support from big business companies everywhere and in 1979 one of these helped the London Festival Ballet to produce *La Sylphide*.

The financial director of the company will prepare an advance budget; a list of all possible expenses. He or she will know how many perfor-

---

Lucette Aldous as Kitri in *Don Quixote* as revived by Rudolf Nureyev. For this version Nureyev mixed original choreography with memories of productions he had experienced in Russia where many of the old ballets are still performed.

Opposite
Alfonso Cata and later Kent Stowell mounted several versions of the classics such as *Swan Lake*, here with Maria Guerrero as Odette, for the small Frankfurt Ballet. Being an opera house company they can enjoy the luxury of long rehearsal times as well as call upon extra performers, not dancers, to play the parts of courtiers or huntsmen.

Above
What comes next? Peter Schaufuss working on a rehearsal of *La Sylphide*. The dancers protect themselves from cramps and cold during rehearsals by wearing woollen or plastic tights. Rehearsals are not the time to worry about looking nice. They are the time for hard work.

---

mances of the new ballet the company hope to give and how much they hope the public will pay to see it. There will be the fees for the designer, lighting expert and choreographer to consider. Any extra costs, such as the fees and expenses of guest artists must also be taken into account. On top of this is the cost of the sets and costumes as well as the everyday running expenses of the company. The financial director will have to bear in mind how many days the company will rehearse—days which will not be producing income at the box-office for the company. And then there will be the printing of programmes, the publicity. . . .

For a two-act ballet with full décor and elaborate costumes, this sum

The studio at the London Festival Ballet headquarters where most of the rehearsals for *La Sylphide* took place. This splendid building was one of the great achievements of Beryl Grey's directorship of the company, a wonderful change from years of working in dingy studios and church halls.

could well be in the region of £80,000 ($175,000). Nearly all of this money will be needed immediately, while the money given by the public will not come in for a long time. This means that a large sum has to be raised in advance from the various sources I have already told you about.

At this time we must not forget the actual ballet! The company will have to have good reasons for performing it and they will have to convince private supporters that the work they have chosen will justify the expense and reflect well on those who support it. For private industry it will be a very good piece of advertising as their name will appear on programmes, posters and advertisements. You will see the same thing happen at big sports events.

The artistic reasons for choosing a ballet are varied. It could be simply that the production of a classic the company dances is past its best. It may have been toured from town to town for many years and small changes of costumes or steps will have added up until it is no longer a good show.

Even a very popular production may be changed once too many people have seen it. A new programme will be needed to keep up the interest of a public who do not want to go back time after time to see an old production.

A ballet may be chosen to fill a gap in the company's repertoire, as was the case with *La Sylphide*. The classic ballets were well represented and there were very good revivals of Diaghilev ballets alongside modern original works. However, apart from an excerpt from *Napoli* and the very attractive one-act ballet *Conservatoire*, there was no major work by the great Danish choreographer Bournonville. As Peter Schaufuss, one of the company's leading dancers, had been brought up in the Bournonville school and 1979 was the hundredth anniversary of Bournonville's death, *La Sylphide* seemed a perfect choice for Festival Ballet.

Once the financial aspect and all the complicated contracts had been settled, work on the actual ballet began. A designer had to be chosen with great care as his or her contribution would be vital to the success of the ballet. Some people have a particular closeness to the romantic style of the ballet and the choice fell on David Walker who had already designed a most beautiful version of *Giselle*, which is of course from the same period of ballet history as *La Sylphide*.

Serious thought had to be given to the casting of dancers for the various roles. Established stars of the company such as Peter Schaufuss and Eva Evdokimova were natural choices for the leading roles of James and the Sylph, but it is important to give young dancers, some completely unknown as yet, a chance in other roles, perhaps as Gurn, Effie or the leading Sylphs.

Away from these practical arrangements the choreographer will have already done a lot of thinking about how the ballet will be danced. Although *La Sylphide* exists in several forms, there is still a lot of room for original ideas.

When Bournonville first created *La Sylphide* he was a brilliant dancer himself, and he made the role of James very important. When he stopped dancing the men who followed him were not as good (some say that Bournonville did not want them to shine as much as he had!) so the role became less important. Over the years other cuts were made, often having nothing to do with the ballet. If the evening was too long, for in those days the ballet would be performed alongside a play and perhaps an opera, cuts would be made. Some of these were restored during this century, but much of the music lay unused for years.

As Bournonville is one of the most respected figures in Denmark, scholars have recently been working in the library of the Royal Theatre and other royal archives and have made important discoveries about the original choreography and the original music. Pieces which had been

La Sylphide exists in several different productions including the one by the Royal Danish Ballet and that produced by Hans Brenaa, the great Bournonville expert for the Scottish Ballet. Niels Kehlet (above) is one of the great Danish male dancers who have danced the role of James.

thought lost have come to light again, as well as some of Bournonville's writings about the ballet.

All Danish dancers are brought up in the tradition of Bournonville and the classes based on his teachings of over one hundred and fifty years ago, are still taught at the Royal Danish Ballet School. This means that a dancer such as Peter Schaufuss, now starting on his first major production, is very familiar with the steps. Students of the school make their first stage appearances in the crowd scenes of Bournonville ballets, such as *Napoli*, and take in the steps almost without realizing it.

Peter Schaufuss remembers being on tour with the Royal Danish Ballet in America as a child. While *La Sylphide* was being performed in the vast Hollywood Bowl, he and other children would copy the comic steps of Madge and the Witches, holding monster ice-creams in their hands instead of brooms! When he came to work on his own production he found that the original steps he had learned for fun in those days, but which have been changed since, came back to him very easily.

Arranging a production is not just a question of putting steps together. There is also a lot of reading to do. It is very useful to go back over the many books which have been written about a ballet to discover as much as possible about how it was performed at different times in the past. It is almost like detective work, finding clues in old newspapers, magazines and books about how costume has changed or how a particular pose used to be.

Very early in the production the musical score will have to be arranged. If the order of the story is being changed and new pieces added, a complete piano score will be made. From this the full orchestral score will be arranged. The conductor or arranger has a problem similar to the choreographer. A sound must be built up which is in keeping with the ballet and will not make it seem too modern. While this is being done rehearsals will take place, using a piano score on a cassette, an invaluable piece of modern equipment, although not as good as working with a pianist who can vary the tempo as needed and give more to the dancer.

By the time the story has been settled and the music arranged to accompany it, work will begin on the steps, with dancers in a studio.

At this point there are yet more practical considerations. Very rarely does a company have the time to work on one ballet alone. It is possible, as with the London Festival Ballet, that they will be performing and working on other ballets at the same time. As a result not every dancer is available all the time, so the ballet master must work out careful schedules with the choreographer.

It is very sensible for instance, to work out all the crowd scenes together, whether they are crowds of Scottish peasants, or crowds of Sylphs. The principal dancers will all learn the roles of James and the Sylph separately, which is just as well as there may be six Jameses and six Sylphs all learning the steps at the same time. Only later will there be individual rehearsals to work on characterization.

As work progresses each separate part becomes more perfect and slowly they are all fitted together. When a big crowd scene is finished, the principal dancers will fit in their parts, first just by walking through the role so that the *corps de ballet* know where they will be, then filling it out with the correct steps. It is all rather like making a film. All the outdoor scenes will be filmed together when the weather is right; all the scenes with the big stars will be filmed together to use as little of their expensive time as possible. Then the editor cuts the film and puts the whole story together. The only difference with the ballet is that the producer, who is usually the choreographer, is working with people and not film, and has to cope with tired and sometimes irritable dancers who do not want to sit around a ballet studio while someone tries to work out which piece goes where!

So, as a sensible and practical step, the Reel in Act One of *La Sylphide* and the main dances for the Sylphs in Act Two will be finished first. These are the parts which will be closest to other productions of the same ballet which you will find in the repertoire of companies in Denmark, Scotland, Canada and America.

Work then begins on the new pieces of choreography which will go with music which has not been used for many, many years. Here the problem will be to create something original and interesting, something which will help the story and make the problems of James more understandable, as well as being in the same style as the rest of the ballet. A new solo for James will show something of his troubled mind over the beautiful Sylph who appears to him. A *pas de trois* for James and Effie, joined by the Sylph while they dance the Reel, shows the audience very clearly how torn he is between these two loves.

Working in the studio on new pieces such as these can be in turn exciting and frustrating. An idea which works perfectly in the mind of the choreographer may not work so well when tried out with the dancers; a simple gesture will not look natural when performed by the ballerina, or a step for the boy will not quite fit in with the music. By a process of trial and error the dances will be built up and then finally polished.

The time will soon come, too soon for some, for the first run-through. This will be the first time that the ballet appears in anything like the shape you will see on the stage. The only difference is that the dancers will be in their funny mixture of practice clothes, without make-up, costumes, lighting or décor to help them create the characters. This way every mistake will show. If they can convince the choreographer now that they not only know the steps, but can also tell the story and show the feelings of the characters, it can only look better on stage.

Usually, however, they cannot and the run-through will be a stop-start affair with a tempo not right here, a few forgotten steps there. The *corps de ballet* may bump into the ballerina or the leading man forget his

David Walker's design for the first act of *La Sylphide*.

entrance. This is the equivalent of the 'rough-cut' in film-making; the time to see if the rhythm of the work is right and if the overall shape looks good. As for the details, it usually means back to the studio the next day to continue the hard, painstaking rehearsal.

By this time the designer will have prepared some first sketches for the sets and costumes. Before starting on these there will be meetings with the choreographer to learn about the practical requirements of the production. A door might have to be in a certain place to fit the action; the fireplace through which the Sylph disappears and the window through which she floats, will have to be planned. These are fixed things around which the designers must create an atmospheric décor. There will also be meetings with the technical director of the company to discuss any limitation that must be coped with. As a company like London Festival Ballet tour much of the time, any set will have to fit several different theatres. In this case the main problem will be with the theatre in which the ballet is to receive its first performance.

The Royal Festival Hall is normally a concert hall with a large platform for an orchestra and a steep bank of seats behind it for a chorus who face out to the audience. From its earliest performances here the ballet company have had to use a temporary stage built over the concert platform area. Some of the front seats are taken out in order to fit their orchestra in, and a huge curtain is hung across the front to make it look like a real theatre. However, backstage it is nothing like one. There is no space at the side or back of the stage. When you leave it you immediately have to climb the steep tiers where the chorus normally sit. The audience see only a beautiful line of Swans coming onto the stage. When the first is on it the last is still somewhere up the stairs. If a dancer leaves the stage on one side and has to reappear on the other, it will mean running up the stairs, along a corridor and back down the other side. This is very different to the life led by companies who have their own theatre, such as the Royal Ballet at Covent Garden, or the New York City Ballet at the State Theater in Lincoln Center.

The designer has the problem of making this very wide but not very deep stage look quite different by the use of clever tricks of perspective. In the case of *La Sylphide* David Walker used the steps themselves to suggest the hills and banks in the woods. Another problem is that none of the scenery can be raised overhead as in a normal theatre. Everything must either be pulled to the side, or designed so that each piece can be folded, taken apart and then carried away from the stage area.

In general designers for the ballet face special problems apart from those unique to the Royal Festival Hall. All the sets have to be kept well back from the dancing area. Small props or items of furniture must be very carefully positioned so that they do not get in the way. Exits and entrances, whether doors or just spaces in the wings (the sides of the stage), must be kept quite clear. It is no use designing a normal-sized door if the whole *corps de ballet* have to go dancing out through it. There is also the problem of colour. It does not matter, indeed it can be an advantage, if the costume of a singer or actor blends with the scenery. In a ballet the character *should* be clearly seen so that every movement can be appreciated and a beautiful line is not spoilt, unless there is some dramatic reason for it.

With *La Sylphide* special thought had to be given to the costumes and the different tartans the dancers would wear. To be very realistic they should probably all wear the same, unless a marriage was taking place between two different clans. However, this could look boring on the stage, so variations have to be devised which still look true. I have seen productions of the ballet where the kilts were painted with invented tartans and the result was not convincing at all. They must also be made of the correct material and be of the right weight so that they move well during the dances. As with all theatrical costumes, they have to be particularly well made to stand the strains of the dancing.

The costume for the Sylphs has to be the romantic *tutu* This was established at the time of the first *La Sylphide* and has been used ever since. It consists of the long white skirt made of tulle which comes to below the knee, and has a tight bodice of satin with perhaps some short sleeves. To match this the ballerina's hair is usually worn drawn back tightly into a bun. It is up to the designer to add the little touches to this basic costume which will turn it into something special.

All the time the steps are being created, the choreographer will be keeping an eye on all these other activities. The choreographer is really like the producer and director of a film combined. They divide the work, one directing the actors, the other arranging the business and the publicity. The choreographer can be creating steps one minute and arranging

David Walker's designs for the leading Sylph.

Opposite
Dancer Nelson Fernandez of Ballet Rambert doing his make-up for a performance. The small sketch shows the body make-up he will use.

Above
Elaborate head-dresses being made in the workshops of the Australian Ballet.

---

a rehearsal schedule another; coping with dancers' problems and then having a meeting with the designer as well as being available for interviews and photocalls to publicize the ballet.

The time will very soon come when the whole production must move into a theatre. Each character will now have a costume which will have involved several costume fittings. This is not the dancer's favourite way of spending time, as it can mean standing like a tailor's dummy for long periods while costumes are pinned, and unpinned if there are problems. They will have practised special hairstyles and how to use any of the intricate decorations which may have been made. Shoes will have been sewn and dyed if they have to match a costume. Character shoes with their stiffer soles and raised heels will have been broken in.

The set will be built by now and assembled by the stage crew. From various studios all over London the different elements will come into place. Unlike a major opera house in Europe or America the companies in Britain do not have the facilities to do everything themselves. They do not have the massive workshops, bigger than industrial concerns, which you would see at the Metropolitan Opera House, for instance. Some companies will specialize in painting the enormous backcloths, a very special technique. It is rather like painting by numbers. The small design created by the designer will be scaled up to the correct size and then

James (Peter Schaufuss) lies asleep while the Sylph (Galina Samsova hovers near him at the beginning of *La Sylphide*.

painted. Some companies are best at making three-dimensional objects, such as moulded trees or houses of the type seen in *Giselle*. And then there are the companies which specialize in making small objects for use in the production—the props. These can range from bunches of flowers and rings and jewellery, to the stuffed pheasants Hilarion brings Giselle.

There will be technical rehearsals on the empty stage to plan how one set can best be taken down and the next one put up. If the stage has no storage space, as with the Royal Festival Hall, the space for each piece of unused scenery has to be planned down to the last detail.

The lighting designer will have made a plan of the production and will be checking that all the lamps are in the correct positions and all the right colour filters have been obtained. There will be a plan of all the cues needed for every change of mood and also a rough plan of the work the follow spot (the beam which shines on the principal characters as they move about) will have to do.

The first dress rehearsal is always the most worrying time for everyone involved. For the dancers there is the obvious problem of doing the right steps and the right actions, which can be difficult as this may be the first time they have danced their role to orchestral accompaniment. I have seen a dancer miss a cue because the music has sounded unfamiliar when played by an orchestra, after having rehearsed it for weeks to only a piano. It is also quite possible that at this moment the choreographer will find that the orchestra is playing at the wrong speeds.

It is very important that the conductor should be present at many rehearsals, even playing the piano for some of them, so that the players will be given the right tempo at orchestra rehearsals. This can be a particular source of trouble as the choreographer may change the tempo from one rehearsal to another. Even after days of rehearsing at one speed, when one section is seen in relation to another, the choreographer may decide that it should be faster or slower. If the conductor is not there, dancers and music may not be together at the dress rehearsal.

Some conductors feel they never can be right. I have heard one ask a dancer, 'How would you like me to play it this time, too fast or too slow?'

In front of the stage, at a table set up in the orchestra stalls, sit the choreographer, the ballet master, the technical director, the lighting designer and the designer of the sets and costumes.

When the cue is given, the orchestra begins the overture and the show is underway for the first time. Rarely does it get far without a problem. If the orchestra plays a few wrong notes, they can be overlooked until the next orchestra rehearsal, but if the curtain rises too soon or too late, it will mean going back a few bars and trying again.

This type of rehearsal can be very difficult for a company such as the London Festival Ballet which does not have its own theatre. If this were taking place in an opera house, for instance, it would be the first of many such rehearsals. I have followed the progress of a production, not more complicated than *La Sylphide*, which had weeks, not days, of stage rehearsal. London Festival Ballet rarely have more than two days, as this

James (Peter Schaufuss) dances a brilliant solo, including these typical Bournonville style jumps, during the celebrations to mark his betrothal to Effie.

means two days when the theatre will not be available for public performances, with the resulting loss of income.

As the dress rehearsal progresses there will be many stops—to discuss the music, or to get a particular solo exactly right. The Sylph will look very unromantic as she dances her solo and at the same time counts aloud the beats of the music for the conductor to get the tempo exactly right.

Concentration may also be spoilt by the presence of photographers filling the front of the orchestra stalls. They do not use flash-lighting, but the combined clicks of their cameras at the high points of a beautiful *pas de deux* can be very distracting. They too have their problems. The stage lighting will almost certainly not be right yet, producing some very odd effects when the colour films are processed. A beautiful group will be spoilt by one costume being incomplete or a charming scene of Sylphs might be spoilt by one of them still wearing her woolly leg warmers. These photographs are vital for publicity and will be the ones you see in newspapers or dance magazines. Although some are posed in studios, the most exciting are usually moments captured in performances.

It is during this rehearsal that any special effects will be tried for the first time, often with disastrous results. *La Sylphide* is one ballet which is full of them. Originally Bournonville devised clever stage machinery to make it look as though the Sylph was flying to a tree-top, or for her to float down from the window sill. Some of these ideas are still in use today, but as modern audiences are used to spectacular effects in films or rock shows, it is sometimes necessary to take a second look at them, or the ballet may look very old fashioned and too much of a period piece. Lifts balanced by weights to raise the Sylph can be replaced by the simple idea of having a boy draped in black lift her up, or even be done away with altogether. To bring her down from her window, Peter Schaufuss decided that it would look just as charming for her to step on a carefully designed pile of old books, rather than wobble as a small lift lowered her down. When she vanishes up the chimney, she is simply pulled up by one of the dancers. Also, this way, there is the added bonus of no machinery to break down.

It is at the rehearsal that the choreographer will see if the ideas which worked in the studio look the same on stage. Perhaps the boy draped in

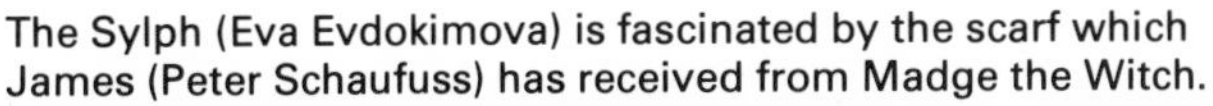
The Sylph (Eva Evdokimova) is fascinated by the scarf which James (Peter Schaufuss) has received from Madge the Witch.

black will be too obvious to the audience, or stepping on the books will not look magical. Now is the time to put things right. In the same way it will be now that the characters get the feel of their costumes; the witch will dance wearing long ragged clothes for the first time and must see that they will not get caught in the scenery. These are small things you might never think of, but they all have to be planned to the last detail to avoid disasters on the first night. For the following day, before the first performance, the ballet master will have made notes from the dress rehearsal which might mean a lot of correction for the dancers. The choreographer will see to all the problems revealed the night before, which need studio rehearsal. In the theatre the stage crew will be working out ways of making the scene-change more quickly and perhaps more quietly. The conductor will be finalizing the correct *tempi* with the orchestra.

In spite of all these problems and tiredness from the long dress rehearsal, the excitement of the first night seems to make everyone do their best. The orchestra suddenly sound wonderful, when the night before they made so many mistakes. The dancers who looked so tired now sparkle with life. The scene-changes are smooth and every stage-trick works. The shallow stage looks deep and mysterious, as the tragic tale of the Sylph and James unfolds.

The audience applaud and cheer. The next day's papers are full of praise for everyone involved. *La Sylphide* is a complete success.

Before the excitement of the season is over, rehearsal schedules are already on the company notice board for the next new production.

A Ballerina's Life - Lynn Seymour

It is very easy to imagine the life of a ballerina in the theatre. You can think of her in her daily class like every other dancer from the corps de ballet *to stars. She may then rehearse a ballet she will perform that evening. The day might be broken up by costume fittings or a photocall for publicity, and there will be many other boring breaks, too short for her to leave the theatre. There may be the excitement of starting a new ballet with a favourite choreographer. And then there is the performance which can make even the most experienced ballerina very nervous. Sometimes it is this nervousness which makes the performance great!*

As you can see, a day like this leaves very little time for a home life. To find out how a ballerina arranges this part of her life—the household chores, the shopping and looking after a family—I spoke to Lynn Seymour. She is a brilliant dramatic ballerina who now creates exciting ballets as well as dancing in them. She has directed a major German ballet company and appeared often on television. In between these activities she has found time to have a family as well.

I began by asking her how she coped with all these activities.

Lynn Seymour: The answer is that I don't sit at home and work everything out myself. If I did I would never get to the theatre! The dancing part of life gives a framework, as so many things are fixed and must be done every day. I know that at a certain time of day there will be a class which I will take. When I was directing a company I sometimes had to teach it as well. I have a performing schedule fairly well in advance from my agent, who handles only my dancing engagements. I will have a plan of when and where I am to be in certain places, perhaps making a guest performance or recording something for a television series such as *The Magic of Dance* which Dame Margot Fonteyn introduced. From this list I can work out in advance what the rehearsals are likely to be. The actual times may change an hour or two, and if a work has been well rehearsed may not be necessary at all. The ballet masters who arrange the rehearsals at the Royal Ballet, for instance, will have an idea of my freelance work and try to arrange things to suit me, but of course they have to keep other

people happy as well. It poses an enormous organizational problem, especially when the other principal dancers have a lot of freelance work as well. If you are with a large company such as the Royal Ballet it may work out that you cannot do everything you want, but your loyalty must be with that company.
Craig Dodd: And the other part of your life?
LS: I surround myself with useful people! Among my friends are my accountant who pays my bills (he even pays me a salary) and a nanny who looks after my three children. I have a travel agency which knows my moves pretty well, and I even subscribe to a problem-solving agency. They find records for me, send flowers or do a million other chores. This way I am left to concentrate on the two most important things—my dancing and my sons.
CD: How have they fitted into your busy life?
LS: Very well indeed. I like having them around either in the theatre or at home. The twins are now old enough to be a great help at home and are wonderful bartenders if I give a party. The little one goes on tour with me and is very used to travel and life in hotels. There are occasional problems such as making sure their schooling isn't interrupted. For instance, on the last long American tour which I made with the Royal Ballet I had to arrange for them to stay with relatives in California and continue their schooling there. This way they weren't harmed and I was able to see them. We spend as much time together at home as we can, but I'm not a homebody. I can cook, but like to do things properly. In any case, the daily schedule I have often doesn't allow time for simple things like shopping, and ordering everything over the telephone isn't fun. I'm not one of those ballerinas who can do four acts of *Swan Lake* and then rush home and cook a dinner. No way. I prefer to come home and rest, or go out and have a good time!
CD: Did the arrival of your sons affect your dancing and your career?
LS: Yes, and only for the best. When my twins were born I was not feeling on top of the world. In fact you can say I was a bit tired of dancing and I wanted to have a family. After they were born I didn't immediately rush back to the theatre! I went back for practical reasons as much as the urge to dance again. Having a baby affects a ballerina physically, and most seem to dance much better after the experience. Emotionally too it must affect the ballerina, but perhaps this is exactly the same for every woman and every family. Dancers can become too involved in dancing and the daily life of the ballet company. A family takes you away from this. Perhaps it brings maturity along with the organizational problems!
CD: Do you think the experience of your early days with the touring company of the Royal Ballet helps you cope with the complicated life you now lead?

LS: Yes, it must. Dancers start work very young and immediately have to cope with lots of practical problems. They are forced to be independent from the start, which makes them very self-reliant. You have to manage the nomadic life—moving from town to town each week, or if you are very unlucky, from day to day. It's up to you to make sure you're there. It's up to you to organize your travel. It's up to you to find somewhere to stay—either a hotel if you can afford it or theatrical digs (lodgings) if you can't. You really are on your own.
CD: Well, not exactly. You are with a whole ballet company most of the time! Does the ballet take over your whole life?
LS: It can. You spend a lot of your youth working in a disciplined way in studios and rehearsal rooms. Once you get into a company as a *corps de ballet* member you seem to spend as much of your time waiting for something to happen as you do actually dancing. Your calls, the times you are needed for rehearsals, can be maddeningly arranged so that you are needed more or less all day, but perhaps in short spells. Leaving the theatre in between the calls is a real chore, as you have to do a few warming up exercises every time you get back. If you don't and you start work 'cold' you run the risk of accidents.

Unless you are lucky enough to share an apartment with a non-dancer, this sort of life means you meet dancers, dancers and more dancers. You might meet the occasional choreographer for light relief! It's not just a question of social life. I think it's very important for young dancers to experience everyday life and to keep up-to-date with theatre, films and books. When I was on tour I always made straight for the local museums, galleries or antique markets. In the end all the experiences have to help your performances, or perhaps to understand what a modern choreographer wants. I am known as a dramatic ballerina, and I am sure that outside experiences have helped my performances of dramatic roles. Perhaps you can be a great Odette in *Swan Lake* leading a life completely involved in the ballet, but to create roles such as the young girl in *The Invitation* or even Juliet, who is such a modern girl, you must have the outside experiences.
CD: When you started ballet classes did you have any idea how things would turn out, that you would be a dramatic ballerina, for instance?
LS: Good heavens, no. I only started to dance because my mother took me to ballet classes. She had wanted to dance herself but had not been allowed to. To make up for this she let me do it, though she wasn't a 'ballet mother' pushing me onto the stage as a career. I was taught in the early years by Svetlanov in Vancouver. He had left Russia via Shanghai with Vera Volkova who was Dame Margot's teacher there. I did the usual school performances and the Sun-Ray Revue but nothing very serious. I did learn to tap, which I think is very important to help children

with rhythm as well as presentation. I only started serious lessons at twelve and two years later came to London to the Sadler's Wells School. It wasn't 'Royal' in those days.

Although being a late starter created problems, these were mostly concerning technique. I think it is important that children be allowed to develop at a natural pace and not be pushed too hard to perform. So many of those who are in the front line of school shows seem to be worn-out before they are of an age to join a ballet company. The same must go for dramatic ability. All children are good actors and have no inhibitions. They can usually laugh or cry with equal ease on the stage. I know that my own talent only flowered when I began to work with choreographers such as Kenneth MacMillan.

CD: This happened soon after you left the Sadler's Wells School?

LS: In the same year. First of all I left the school, in 1956, to dance in the

Lynn Seymour in two scenes from *Anastasia*, one of the great dramatic ballets which Kenneth MacMillan created for her: (Below) As the young Anastasia, daughter of the Tsar, with her parents, sisters and the sinister Rasputin; (Right) Rasputin becomes a part of her nightmare when she is Anna Anderson, the woman who claims to be Anastasia—only survivor of the Imperial family which was massacred during the Russian Revolution.

operas in Sadler's Wells. Then I joined the Royal Ballet touring company along with dancers such as Christopher Gable. Kenneth MacMillan told me that he saw me rehearsing Peter Wright's ballet *The Blue Rose* and knew immediately that I was the girl he wanted for his ballet *The Burrow*, a dramatic work based on the very sad, but very beautiful, story *The Diary of Anne Frank*.

CD: Can you explain your very close working relationship with Kenneth MacMillan?

LS: After he had seen me and we had worked together, we found that we thought exactly on the same wavelength. Kenneth told me long afterwards that he found that I almost anticipated what he wanted, that I seemed to know instinctively what he was about to do. I suppose my way of moving and the shape of my body were exactly what he was looking for. You know how different choreographers prefer different types. George Balanchine, for instance, likes his wonderful long-legged ballerinas, almost the very opposite of me. My way of moving was so near what he wanted that even now, when other great dancers perform roles he created on me, people say that they are reminded of me. Of course they dance individually and brilliantly. It's not that they copy me. It's just that those shapes are in Kenneth's choreography. When I eventually danced *Manon*, I was told that it looked as though it was made for me. *Romeo and Juliet* was made for me, with Christopher Gable as Romeo, though the first performance was given by Margot Fonteyn and Rudolf Nureyev. Even now I am told that the ballroom solo, for instance, reminds audiences of me! When it comes to creating actual steps in the studio, it is easier for me to tell you what Kenneth doesn't do. He does not arrive with ideas firmly worked out and then teach us how to do them. In fact in the early rehearsals of his ballets he hardly uses the names of steps at all. He just suggests general movements, like run there, fall this way, bend that way, until we have caught the spirit of the music. When we have finished blocking in the pieces of dance, rather like painting in the flat areas of a picture, we start to put in the light and shade. General movements become particular steps until they build up into a sequence such as an *enchaînement* or a whole *pas de deux*.

CD: You were so close to Kenneth MacMillian that you left the Royal Ballet to go to Berlin with him.

LS: This was an important time for me. It seemed almost inevitable, and looking back I think it was wise. It was the time when my twins were born, and Kenneth made a new ballet for me. This was the one-act version of *Anastasia* about the lady who claimed to be the last surviving daughter of the Russian Tsar killed during the Revolution of 1917. This was to become the last act of the full-length version which was later produced by the Royal Ballet. The character of Anna Anderson, alone in a hospital with her memories, was perfectly developed by Kenneth. I remember the first rehearsals well. We had talked about the role before, and to establish the way Anna was looking for her identity he opened the ballet by having her walk around as though fascinated by the floor. Kenneth thought that this was the only firm thing, the only real thing, in her life at that moment. You can see how the character comes first. The steps follow later.

CD: Your twins are now old enough to think about dancing themselves.

LS: Yes they are, but if they are thinking about it they aren't showing it. They know the life of a dancer very well, having been to so many places with me. Perhaps it's put them off the idea! I am not going to push them into ballet, even though there is always a shortage of boys, and most can make a fair career. One of them has now taken up judo at school, and as long as they stay athletic and active there is always the chance they might just decide to dance. As you know, boys can start much later than girls, so we just have to wait and see.

Training a Star - George de la Pena

George de la Pena is the young star of the film Nijinsky *in which he appears as the greatest male dancer in the history of ballet; a dancer of outstanding technique and special personality. Playing such a famous person, who is still remembered by a few people in the ballet and whose legend has grown over the years presents special problems. Nijinsky began his training in St Petersburg at the Imperial School.*

I started by asking George de la Pena how he began his dance training.

George de la Pena: I didn't set out to be a dancer at all. At first I wanted to attend the High School of the Performing Arts in New York to study music. That course was full and I was advised to enrol for the dance course. The intention was to change over once I was in the school. As you see I didn't.
Craig Dodd: Briefly, what sort of training did you receive there?
GP: It's a high school like any other, except the emphasis is on the arts. It teaches the usual academic subjects alongside your first subject, say dance or drama, so you get a complete education. My main subject was dance so about half of my time was spent doing the usual dance studies. The other half was given over to general subjects including music and drama.
CD: Why and when did you move to the School of American Ballet?
GP: It was only for the last year of my training, before joining American Ballet Theater (ABT), that I attended the School of American Ballet (SAB) alone. For three years I attended both schools. I went to SAB, I suppose, because it's the best school, the one Mr Balanchine created when he first came to New York in the 'thirties. It supplies dancers to the New York City Ballet as well as many other companies across America and in Europe. It also has an impressive faculty of teachers.
CD: Why did you attend both schools?
GP: Well, the American system is not like the British. The SAB is a school to produce performers. It's not like a local ballet school which teaches people how to dance. There everything you do is intended to

guarantee you turn out as a professional dancer. As a result they teach nothing other than dance. This can make a problem for young students and their parents. They have to pay for two schools, one for general studies and then the SAB. The student has to work really hard to fit both courses in, especially as at SAB dance comes first and you can't just miss classes if they clash with something else. So I worked on at the high school for three years and then at Hunter College for my last year.

CD: Were there any problems when you first joined SAB?

GP: Not with the dancing. I came to the school rather late, I must have been around sixteen. Most of the students had been there much longer, some since they were kids. It was the general atmosphere which worried me most. Coming from a school which mixed the subjects and where the pupils' main object wasn't getting into a company or onto the stage at all costs, I found the atmosphere very competitive. Life can be very hard for students at the school, with the constant pressure to succeed. I was helped a great deal by the principal teacher for the boys, Stanley Williams.

CD: Well, I first saw you there in 1974 and you seemed as competitive as the rest!

GP: I promise you I didn't start out that way!

CD: Could you give me a brief idea of what a day at SAB is like?

GP: Well, my day was different as I started late. If you start your training at the school, which I didn't, I think you get to do class twice a week. This is enough when you are only nine or so as the exercises then are very simple and repetitive. Classes are later in the afternoon to allow time for general education. As you go up grades, dance takes more of the day and the student has to work hard to fit things in. Also by this time they will have been through several gradings and anyone not dedicated enough will have been weeded out. If you live through these years you know you really want to dance!

CD: And for the older boys?

GP: By the time they are fourteen or so they will be having their daily class at 12.30 with Stanley Williams or Andrei Kramarevsky. Occasionally a guest teacher from the company, such as Peter Martins, would take a class. After a break there are the specialist classes such as *adagio* to learn how to partner your ballerina and do other double work. Later in the evening, at 5.30, there is the men's class at which dancers from the company, or international stars visiting New York, will be present. This is always good for the students.

CD: What about the girls' training?

GP: Well, I'm not an expert on that, but from what I can remember their day will go something like this: ballet class at 10.30 followed by different classes according to their grade. Some will do a *pointe* work class with Alexandra Danilova (a lot of people will have seen her as the teacher and coach in *The Turning Point*). She also gives a very popular variation class when they learn something from the classic repertoire. They will also be joining the boys for the *adagio* class. In the evening there's a further class for the more advanced girls.

CD: Do the students do any actual performances?

GP: There is the annual school performance and work for that will have gone on throughout the year. Usually it's a mixture of pieces from the company repertoire and ballets made specially for it.

CD: Did you take part?

GP: Yes I did. I danced the 'Bluebird' *pas de deux* from *The Sleeping Beauty* as well as in a new ballet by Richard Tanner.

CD: And then you didn't join the New York City Ballet. Isn't that unusual for such a good male dancer?

GP: Right. It's difficult to look back and say exactly why I didn't join. As you say any good boys usually go straight into the company, although I can think of one or two others who didn't. Girls have a much bigger problem. To get in they have to be good, very good. Honestly, I don't think I made any special effort to join. I didn't even talk to Mr Balanchine about it. An offer came from the American Ballet Theater which seemed good at the time, so I took it.

CD: What were your first performances with ABT and how did things develop?

GP: I got some very good roles early on. To give you a couple of examples. I danced the part of the second sailor in Jerome Robbins' *Fancy Free*, you know, the ballet about three sailors on leave which was turned into the big film musical *On the Town*. My part was first played by John Kriza, one of the first great male stars of the American ballet after the last war. I also danced the role of the Lover in Antony Tudor's *Lilac Garden* (*Jardin aux Lilas*) and worked with Tudor on it. He has always had a close relationship with ABT since he came over from Britain before the war and many of his best ballets were made there, including, of course, *Pillar of Fire* for Nora Kaye who is now working on my film.

CD: The film. How did you get the part?

GP: I don't know! I'm sure many much better-known dancers than I were the first names thought of. Fortunately Nora Kaye and Herbert Ross knew my work very well. Nora had been a ballerina with ABT as well as being a director. Both had a good eye for ballet on film, having made *The Turning Point* together with Lesley Browne. She appears in this film, too, as my wife Romola. Although I'm slighter than Nijinsky, who had a very stocky and muscular body, to judge from photographs, I do have a slightly 'oriental' look, the same as his. And in spite of my name, which is my mother's, I have Russian blood. My family name is pretty unpronounceable!

CD: Any doubts about portraying such a famous dancer?
GP: Not really. I am trying to create an impression of Nijinsky in the film. It's about his whole life, not just his dancing, although there is a lot of it. The important thing for me was to catch the character either as himself or in his roles. There's no point in trying to jump as high.
CD: Did you do much preparation for the role?
GP: You mean reading and not dance training, I suppose. No, I didn't. I've read the important books, the biography and the diaries, but I think it's important to take your ideas from the script and not to arrive in the studio with your own idea of Nijinsky's character worked out in detail.
CD: Any problems before you got to the cameras?
GP: Not really problems, just things to work at. The most obvious hurdle is to get your voice sorted out. Obviously dancers don't breathe the same way as actors, so voice training is needed. I still do my classes. When I saw a test of me actually talking, it wasn't what I expected , but it didn't sound too peculiar. I didn't have any problems with learning the lines or the script, which is by Hugh Leonard who has written the books of several successful Broadway shows.
CD: Did the acting part come naturally?
GP: Yes. It's not the same as ballet acting which is bigger and broader. I even found that improvizing scenes and occasionally inventing dialogue came naturally too. For instance, the scene where Nijinsky rehearses his ballet *The Rite of Spring* is pretty much improvized.
CD: How many of Nijinsky's roles do you dance and what sort of preparations did you make?
GP: Let me see, we do either complete or in excerpt, *Spectre de la Rose, Petrushka, Schéhérazade, Afternoon of a Faun, Carnaval* and *Jeux*. My preparations were much the same as you'd expect for a stage performance. I had danced *Petrushka* before, with ABT, but the other roles were new. Fortunately everyone working on the film was a great help.
CD: Who helped you with the roles you hadn't danced before?
GP: So many people. First of all you have to remember that all the dancers taking part were very experienced. The *corps de ballet* and soloist roles were taken by dancers from London Festival Ballet. They have enormous experience in dancing the Diaghilev ballets. Their ballet master, Vassilie Trunoff, is expert at rehearsing them. Nicholas Beriosov, father of Svetlana Beriosova, had produced *Petrushka* and *Schéhérazade* for the company and he helped a lot too. Irina Baronova helped with all the roles. She was one of the baby ballerinas who had incredible publicity

---

George de la Pena as Nijinsky dancing the role of the Faun.

with the Ballets Russes companies which tried to follow Diaghilev in the 'thirties.

CD: Were any other personalities of the Diaghilev era brought in to help?

GP: I talked to many, but in particular to the wonderful Anton Dolin. He's so full of life and bright ideas. He also appears in the film—a direct link with Diaghilev for whom he danced in the 'twenties.

CD: Does filming ballet present any special problems?

GP: The main problem seems to be that there are no rules about the way you should do things. Different ballets were approached in different ways. It's an exhausting business with the very early starts, and time always has to be found for the ballet class, or just a warm-up. There are technical difficulties which seem enormous when you first start, but you get used to them. By the time we were filming we all knew our roles and then had to place them for the cameras. This is really fairly routine work and not unlike a normal ballet rehearsal. Even stopping and starting is a bit like working with a choreographer or teacher on a ballet. This can be a worry when you're doing a complete role and are building the character up nicely. If you are doing *Petrushka* in the theatre you get carried along by the non-stop action, the reaction of the audience and the build-up of that fantastic music. On film you're playing it cold. I just hope it looks dramatic up there on the screen.

CD: Are all the ballets shown as we would see them in a theatre?

GP: Not exactly. If you sit in one seat in the theatre you get one view. If you're in a bad seat you get one long bad view. I think if everything was filmed from the best seat, centre orchestra stalls, it could be boring. What the director did was to film everything with five cameras in different positions. He and his editor will then cut the film to give you the best idea of the ballet being performed, mixing close-ups with whole scenes as well as tracking shots which follow the action across the stage. On the whole the ballet scenes are uninterrupted so you see complete pieces. Of course we cannot show every ballet complete purely on grounds of time, and in any case there is the complex story of Nijinsky, Diaghilev and Romola to be told. It is a film about the complete person, not just the dancing, and these dramatic scenes gave me as much pleasure as the dancing.

CD: And what next?

GP: I prefer to see how this film works out first. While we are talking, the film is only just being completed, so it will be a few months before it appears in cinemas. Till then I am committed to the film. It's not only dancing and acting. I have to be available for publicity and interviews, just like this one. It would be nice to dance with ABT again and I could make guest appearances, I suppose. In fact, I would very much like to dance with Gelsey Kirkland whom I admire greatly, but I don't want to rush into anything. I have a two-film contract, but what the second will be I do not know. I'm fascinated by the rest of the Nijinsky story which continues long after the end of this film, but that would be a purely acting role. I have been approached with several other projects and I'm interested in teaching. But at the moment I am just doing class, keeping myself in shape. I'm in no hurry.

The Ballets

There are now so many ballet companies, large and small, that you stand a very good chance of seeing many of the most famous ballets such as *Swan Lake, Nutcracker* or *Giselle*. The special treasures of companies such as the Royal Danish Ballet may present you with more difficulty as they are not able to tour the world as they would like, due to their commitments at home. Some of their ballets, those by the great Bournonville, are now being danced by other companies and it cannot be long before every major company has something by Bournonville in its repertory.

Some of the small modern ballets are not so widely performed, but you may have a chance to see them on television. Most do not have stories, so I have included only one or two examples; they show perfectly how ballet is to be seen and not to be written about. In the case of the 'story' ballets, you should always remember that the story is just a peg on which to hang wonderful dance. This is why many of the old, long passages of mime have been swept away and choreographers leave a lot more to your imagination.

Another word of warning! Although I am going to tell you the stories of many of the classical ballets, you may well go to see one in a theatre only to find that it is not exactly what I lead you to expect! The reasons for this can be many. It might be a simple technical problem. Most classical ballets need large numbers of dancers who have to be Swans in one act and elaborately dressed courtiers in another. Obviously only the very big companies, such as the Bolshoi in Moscow, have enough people for each dancer to take only one role. This means you may see fewer Swan maidens than you expect, especially in a production which tries to make the whole evening shorter by letting the first act of *Swan Lake* continue into the second act with only a short pause. Imagine the rush backstage as the girls (it is usually the girls who suffer) have to dash to their dressing rooms, taking the court headdresses out of their hair while still in the corridors. Having been peasant girls celebrating Prince Siegfried's birthday in the first act, they must quickly change into Swans for the second. This means not only changing from a simple peasant dress to the classical *tutu*, but also changing their hair-style to match and putting on a very pale, mysterious make-up. If you watch a performance from behind the scenes, you will nearly always see the last Swans making a mad rush to the stage, almost running to the wings where they have to make the sudden change to the slow entry of the Swans. Having performed this act beautifully, they then have to reverse the process to put on elaborate national costumes, perhaps heavy furs and brocades, to take part in the ballroom scene which follows. If that were not enough, they then have to become Swans again for the last act, when Odette and Siegfried throw themselves into the lake to overcome the power of the evil magician Von Rothbart.

Productions will differ in many other ways. Perhaps the producer and choreographer see the story in a completely different way. They may want to bring it up to date and use modern settings and costumes. They may feel that part of the story can be made to show something that is happening in the world today. There may even be political reasons for change, which you might notice if you ever have the opportunity to see a Russian production of *Swan Lake*. Sad endings are not popular in the USSR and the people who are in the right, in this case Odette and Siegfried, must defeat the evil powers represented by Von Rothbart. So the last scene shows Odette transformed back from Swan Queen to her earthly role of beautiful Princess. I'm certainly not in favour of this; I like good old-fashioned drama!

And now to the ballets. The stories appear in the order in which the ballets were created, starting with the ever-popular tale of love and confusion in a French farmyard.

La Fille Mal Gardée

This ballet is one of the oldest still performed, although the versions you are most likely to see date from much later. The first production was by Jean Dauberval in Bordeaux, France, in 1789. The idea developed in his mind after he glimpsed an engraving in a shop window. It showed an angry lady chasing a young man from her farm, while her pretty daughter looked on. Dauberval brought this picture to life and made the people very realistic. He also used popular tunes of the day as in the music for the farmers going about their work and bringing in the harvest, and for the two lovers as they finally defeat Widow Simone's efforts to keep them apart.

The production of 1789 has been lost and the most popular versions today are based on performances given in Paris in 1837 and Russia in 1885. The music differs too, but we can be fairly sure that both of these

David Roxander (Alain) is so busy partnering Karen Kain (Lise) that he does not see Frank Augustyn (Colas) stealing kisses in the National Ballet of Canada's production of Ashton's *La Fille Mal Gardée*.

productions contained many memories of the first one.

This ballet is important in ballet history as it was the first to show real people on the stage. Before this the stories had always been about mythological tales of gods and goddesses—all very serious and lacking in fun.

Here is the story of Sir Frederick Ashton's version which is performed in Canada, Australia, Sweden, Germany and, of course, by the Royal Ballet in Britain for whom it was created. It varies in small details from the version danced in Russia and America, but the main story of Lise and Colas, the two lovers, is very much the same in all productions.

At daybreak on the farm of Widow Simone the cock and his hens dance to welcome the day. Lise comes from the farmhouse to see if Colas, the young farmer she loves, is near. She cannot see him anywhere so she ties a lovers' knot in pink ribbon as a sign for him. On his way to harvest Colas stops at the farm with his fellow harvesters, but when they leave he stays behind and finds the ribbon.

Lise comes from the house, sure she has heard Colas, but cannot find him until he surprises her. Unfortunately their meeting is interrupted by a furious Widow Simone, just out of bed with her curlers still in her hair. She chases him away, throwing her potted plants after him. To take her mind off Colas, Lise is set to work churning butter, but Colas soon sneaks back to join her at her work. He tries to help, but is soon tired and rests his head on Lise's shoulder. They dance together, playfully, with Lise's ribbons. She uses them to rein Colas like a horse and then they wind the ribbons around their bodies to form a beautiful love knot. Lise's friends arrive and she tries to follow them to the fields. Unfortunately she is once more caught by Widow Simone who is determined that she shall stay behind to meet rich Farmer Thomas and his simple son, Alain. She plans to arrange a marriage which will bring Lise a great fortune and cannot understand why Lise insists on marrying for love. Once more Lise tries to run away and Widow Simone catches her and puts her over her knee. As she is about to spank her, Farmer Thomas arrives, much to the Widow's embarrassment. Alain, clutching his red umbrella, dances clumsily for them, but Lise is not interested. She does not have to see more of Alain, as now the pony cart arrives to take them off to harvest.

On the way to the harvest Lise's mother points out the very grand house she can hope to have if she marries Alain. He is following with Lise's friends who have put ribbons in his mouth and pretend he is a horse pulling a carriage. They are followed by Colas who brings wine for the harvesters and does a brilliant dance anticipating his meeting with Lise.

Led by the strutting cock and the hens they all arrive in the field where the harvesters are working. As noon strikes they stop in the midday heat for their meal. Widow Simone makes Lise dance with Alain, but he is so stupid that he does not notice Colas joining in and stealing kisses while he concentrates on his careful partnering. Soon he is distracted by Lise's friends, leaving the two lovers to dance together. The ever-watchful Widow suddenly notices that Lise is no longer in the field and sets off to look for her. Lise's friends take her mind off the lovers by asking her to dance a clog dance. At first she refuses, but she does not take much encouragement to show off her clever footwork.

As the harvesters dance round the maypole a storm breaks and the heavy winds and a thundery storm force them back to their homes. The cock and hens are blown around the field; Lise and Colas find a quiet moment together before a second outburst blows Alain high into the sky hanging from his red umbrella.

Back home in their large farmhouse Widow Simone and Lise dry themselves. To keep off chills Simone puts a yellow neckerchief on Lise, keeping the nicer, red one for herself. She gives Lise the wool to hold while she spins, but she soon nods off to sleep. Lise tries to steal the key as she knows Colas is outside, but even asleep Simone knows what is happening. The best Lise can do is to spend a brief moment with Colas as he looks over the top of their great two-part door. As he swings her gently in the air Simone wakes and Lise pretends to be dancing. Simone cannot understand it, but doesn't have the time to investigate as the harvesters have now brought in the corn to dry and must collect their pay.

As soon as she is alone Lise dreams of the life she hopes to have with Colas; of their wedding and the family they will raise. As she pretends to play with and teach the children, Colas jumps out from under the corn. She is very embarrassed to think that he has seen her little daydream. He soon consoles her and as a token of love they exchange scarves, Colas giving her his red one. They hear Widow Simone returning and Lise tries to hide Colas, but the only place possible is upstairs in her bedroom. Simone notices that Lise is wearing a different scarf and is sure that Colas is in the house. She looks high and low, but cannot find him anywhere. She then sends Lise up to her bedroom to change into her most beautiful dress ready to meet Farmer Thomas and Alain who are coming to sign the marriage settlement. She cannot understand why Lise does not want to go upstairs and finally drags her up, pushes her into the bedroom and locks the door.

Farmer Thomas arrives with the village lawyers and the documents are signed. Alain is then given the key to Lise's bedroom, but the thought that she is finally to be his bride is too much for him and he falls down the stairs several times before he finally gets the key in the lock. He opens the door only to find Lise in Colas's arms. Farmer Thomas is furious and tears up the documents and stamps on them. Simone pleads with him, but he leaves taking his sad little son home with him.

Widow Simone is so cross to see the prospect of a great fortune fade away that she refuses to give Lise her blessing to marry Colas. Lise's friends plead with her and she finally sees that the two young people are truly in love. She gives her blessing and the villagers, Lise and Colas dance out, singing as they go.

In the last quiet moments there is the sound of a window opening. Alain climbs through and looks around the room. Suddenly he spots his beloved red umbrella, forgotten during the earlier drama. Clutching it in his arms, he dances out happily.

La Sylphide

This was the first complete ballet from the Romantic era, though not the first romantic ballet. When used in this way the word 'romantic' refers to the romance of far away mysterious places and equally mysterious supernatural beings, not to love stories. In *Robert the Devil* Marie Taglioni had danced as a ghostly Abbess, leading her nuns through haunted cloisters. In the new ballet, *La Sylphide*, created for her by her father, she was a Sylph, a wood spirit, who is in love with a human being, James. He sees her as his ideal woman.

The ballet you are most likely to see today is not an exact copy of the first production in Paris in 1832. It will most probably be a version of the one Auguste Bournonville made about four years later in Copenhagen. He used his memories of the original production, but as he could not afford to use the original music, he commissioned a new score from the twenty year old Baron Hermann von Løvenskjold. This is a very important piece of ballet music as it contains many new ideas for the period. For instance the Sylph has her own theme tune which appears throughout the ballet, and the overture tells a little story of its own, bringing together different themes you will hear later in the ballet.

The ballet also has a deeper meaning than appears at first sight, and is very symbolic. The Sylph represents the fantasy of young James, his ideal woman. The very earthy Effie is his human love. He chases his fantasy, but when he catches it, it dies. It is almost another way of saying that if you could make your wildest dreams come true you might well be very disappointed—rather like meeting your favourite ballerina, so magical and ethereal on stage, only to find her concerned with shopping and household chores in between acts.

James is a young Scottish farmer who is due to be married to the charming, lively Effie. While waiting for the celebrations to begin, he sleeps in his big armchair, unaware that the Sylph is hovering behind him. She dances around him, showing her simple and playful personality and her love for him. She kisses him and he wakes suddenly. He tries to catch the Sylph but she always manages to elude his grasp. She finally escapes, as light as a puff of smoke, up the chimney. James is captivated by her charm, but still mystified about who she is as he dozes back to sleep.

Effie arrives with her friends and kisses James. He wakes suddenly once more and reaches out to grasp her. Effie does not understand that he thinks it is the Sylph once more and is disappointed that he does not seem happy to see her. James's friend Gurn is also in love with Effie and angry that he must lose her to the young farmer. While the group are dancing and James presents Effie with a beautiful tartan which will be part of her wedding costume, they do not notice Madge, a witch, coming in to sit by the fire. When James does see her by his hearth he is angry and tries to throw her out, but Gurn and the others beg for her to stay. She is very grateful to them and agrees to tell their fortunes. She predicts, perhaps out of spite, that Effie will marry Gurn and not James. This is too much for James and this time he really does throw her out of his house. During the general celebrations the Sylph appears once more and dances through the crowd. When James is left alone, as the girls take Effie away to put on her wedding clothes, the Sylph appears through the window to dance with James. As they do Gurn sneaks in and sees them. They hear him carelessly closing the door. James hides the Sylph under a large tartan rug on his chair. Gurn rushes back in with the others and rips away the tartan, pointing to the Sylph. But she has vanished and they all think that Gurn is seeing things. There is only Effie's piece of tartan on the chair.

As the celebrations take place the Sylph once more appears to James and begs him to follow her to the woods. At first he refuses, but when she brings him his cap he grasps it and follows her. As the exciting reel comes to an end and the group separates to drink the health of the young couple, they cannot find James.

Gurn runs into the forest to look for him and once again sees him with the Sylph. This time the clansmen are not so sure and think he might be telling the truth after all. Effie tries to run into the forest after James, but her mother consoles her as she sinks to the ground, her wedding celebrations ruined and her love lost.

Deep in the forest Madge and her coven of witches are already plotting against James. Madge will not forgive him for the way he treated her and plans the worst revenge. She will give him a magic scarf which has been swirled in a terrible potion. He will believe that this will help him catch his elusive Sylph, but in reality it will kill her.

James runs after the Sylph and finally catches her in a beautiful glen with a small waterfall. The Sylph dances for him, bringing him water to drink, carefully cupped in her hands. She calls on her fellow Sylphs to come and dance for him. James is entranced by their magic world, but no matter how hard he tries, he cannot catch his love.

As James follows the Sylph into the woods, leaving his cap behind, Gurn and the others come into the glen looking for him. Madge sees Gurn and convinces him that he should not tell the others he has found the hat. She is concerned that she should make her prophecy come true.

Madge lingers in the glen in wait for James. She has the poisoned scarf hanging from her belt to attract his attention. When he comes he sees it and immediately thinks it would be a perfect gift to attract the Sylph. Madge refuses his money, but tells him that she will give it to him as it is a way of catching the Sylph. She shows him how to wind it around the Sylph's arms. James is overjoyed that at last his true love is almost within his grasp.

When he shows the scarf to the Sylph she is immediately enthralled by it. James dances, waving the scarf high above his head as though to tantalize her. Finally he tells her that she may have it and asks her to kneel. He winds it around her outstretched arms and as he does the cold chill of death steals over her. She stands on tiptoe as though wanting to fly, but she cannot as her wings wither and fall away. She collapses into the arms of her sister Sylphs. They unwind the painful scarf to enable her to take a last few faltering steps before she dies.

James is left alone, totally shattered by her death. His anguish is interrupted only by Madge who shows him the wedding procession of Effie and Gurn passing in the distance, before she stands over him, gloating. He has lost everything.

Giselle

The short Romantic age produced only one other ballet which is still performed today. That was *Giselle*. Produced in 1841, it gave the ballerina one of her greatest roles and it is often said that by the time a ballerina is mature enough to present the character, she is too old to dance it. In the first act she must be the simple peasant girl, wildly in love, and in the second a ghostly Wili, a creature more menacing than a Sylph.

Giselle lives in a small village deep in the forest, near to the vineyards. In the distance can be seen the castle of the Duke of Silesia. She is loved by a gamekeeper, Hilarion, who often brings her presents of game caught in the woods. She, however, is in love with a mysterious visitor to the village, called Loys. She does not know that he is really Prince Albrecht escaping from court life.

One day Albrecht visits the village with his squire, Wilfred, and hides his sword and cape in a small house, not realizing that Hilarion has seen him there. He knocks on Giselle's door and then hides. She rushes out, sure it is Loys, but cannot see him. He blows her kisses from his hiding place, but still she cannot find him. As she returns to her home, thinking she must have been hearing the wind blowing through the trees, she bumps into him. He takes her hand and they dance together. They rest for a moment and he tells Giselle that he will always love her. To make sure Giselle picks a flower and plays he loves me, he loves me not, with the petals. She is unhappy when she counts and finds that he will not love her and throws the flower to the ground and rushes away. Albrecht picks it up, quickly throws away one petal, and then convinces her that she has miscounted. She is overjoyed and they dance happily together. Hilarion arrives and tries to claim Giselle's attention, but with a very regal gesture Albrecht commands him to leave.

Giselle is unhappy at this unpleasantness, but they are soon distracted by the arrival of the grapepickers and their friends. Giselle is very fond of dancing and joins in. Her mother comes out to watch and is horrified to find Giselle dancing. She reminds her about her poor health and as an extra warning tells them all the story of the Wilis who haunt the forest. They are the spirits of maidens who die before their wedding day, who dance in the forest and condemn anyone who crosses their path to dance to death.

When they leave to harvest the grapes, Hilarion takes the opportunity to break into Albrecht's hut. In it he finds the sword with its royal crest. He hears a hunting horn in the distance and runs into the forest to hide.

Wilfred rushes into the clearing to warn Albrecht that a hunting party, led by the Duke, has decided to rest in the village. He cannot find him, but in any case it would be too late as the grand party enter, led by the

Margaret Barbieri as Giselle and Alain Dubreuil as Albrecht in the second act of the Royal Ballet production of *Giselle*.

Duke and his daughter, Bathilde, who is engaged to Albrecht.

Giselle's mother and the other villagers offer the party refreshments and two villagers dance for them. Giselle is overawed by the fine dresses and touches the hem of Bathilde's heavily decorated robe. Bathilde speaks kindly to her and gives her a necklace. In return Giselle offers to dance, much to the consternation of her mother.

The hunting party go into Giselle's house to rest. Hilarion comes from his hiding place and compares the crest on the sword he has found with the one on the hunting horn the party have left hanging over the door. He now has definite proof that the so-called Loys is no simple peasant. He must be of royal blood. As he is about to sound the horn to call the party the harvesters appear with their big baskets of grapes and he has to wait. They celebrate a very good harvest and crown Giselle Queen of the Vintage. As she dances happily, Hilarion can wait no longer and challenges Albrecht with the sword. Albrecht swears that Hilarion is wrong and only causing trouble. But it is too late. Hilarion blows on the hunting horn and brings the party from the house. They are surprised to see Albrecht there and Bathilde immediately goes to him and embraces him. Giselle intervenes and tells Bathilde that she is engaged to Albrecht. Bathilde says that this is not possible and shows her the ring which Albrecht has given her. Giselle tears the necklace Bathilde gave her from her neck.

Giselle is completely heartbroken and becomes almost mad. She staggers from group to group not knowing where she is. She relives some of her happy moments with Albrecht repeating part of the joyful dance she did not so long ago. Suddenly she remembers how she tested their love with a flower and as she moves across the clearing, she touches the sword which Hilarion has thrown to the ground. She tries to kill herself, but Albrecht takes it from her grasp in time. As her gestures become more frantic, she runs first to Albrecht and then to her mother's arms where her weak heart gives way to the shock and she dies.

Albrecht realizes he has been the cause of her death, but angrily shows Hilarion what his jealousy has led to.

Giselle is buried deep in the forest, the haunt of the Wilis and their Queen, Myrtha. Hilarion comes into the forest late at night to find the grave, but like the other gamekeepers who work in this part, he is frightened by the menacing atmosphere. They feel the presence of the Wilis flying through the trees. The atmosphere is so frightening that they leave just before Myrtha enters. She dances coldly around her domain, calling in her Wilis from the surrounding darkness. They dance to Myrtha's orders in front of Giselle's grave and Myrtha calls Giselle from her grave, wearing the white dress and veil of a Wili. At Myrtha's order she walks to the centre of the group, head bowed. She dances, turning round and round as though hypnotized by Myrtha's power, leaving the clearing with the other Wilis when Myrtha hears the sound of someone approaching.

Albrecht enters, bearing flowers to lay on Giselle's grave. As he kneels, deep in thought, Giselle appears to him as though in a vision. He tries to grasp her, but she always passes through his arms and he can touch her only briefly as she flies through the air. After this fleeting vision he is left with only the flowers Giselle has plucked and thrown to him. He follows her into the forest.

Hilarion returns to the grave with Myrtha and the Wilis in pursuit. They capture him and in spite of his pleas Myrtha orders that he be thrown into the lake after he has been exhausted by dancing. The line of Wilis take him to the lake and return with Albrecht in their power. He too begs for mercy, but again Myrtha refuses. Giselle pleads on his behalf, but Myrtha takes no notice. To protect Albrecht, Giselle takes him to the cross on her grave which weakens the power of the Wilis. But this is their domain and their power must win. Albrecht is forced to dance to the point of exhaustion and then commanded to dance on until he collapses to the ground almost dead. Though Myrtha still orders his death, Giselle's actions have delayed it long enough for dawn to break. With daybreak the power of Myrtha and the Wilis fades for another night, as does the vision of Giselle. Albrecht follows her to her grave and tries to stop her returning to the cold earth, but the power of death is too great and he is left alone with his grief and only a few flower petals which Giselle has scattered over him.

Napoli

This is not a ballet you will see very often in its complete form, although it is still danced regularly in Denmark where it was first created. You might, however, see the last act which is full of glorious opportunities for young dancers to shine and sometimes includes the charming *pas de deux* from another ballet by Bournonville, *Flower Festival at Genzano*.

This ballet is important as it was one of the very first to use character and national dances and was made nearly thirty years before *Coppélia*, in 1842.

Teresina is a pretty young girl who lives in Naples. She is so beautiful and full of life that three suitors wish to marry her: the macaroni and

---

Elaine MacDonald as Teresina in the Scottish Ballet production of *Napoli* by Bournonville.

lemonade sellers and the handsome young fisherman, Gennaro. Her ambitious mother naturally prefers the businessmen, but Teresina really loves Gennaro.

When the fishermen return with a good catch, Gennaro once more asks Teresina's mother if he may marry her. This time the mother does not say no so firmly which pleases both the lovers.

On the busy quayside a monk mingles with the crowd, asking for alms. The lovers give generously. In spite of the mother's acceptance of Gennaro the two old businessmen will still not leave Teresina alone and they try to make trouble by pointing out that Gennaro is flirting with an attractive girl who has come to buy his fish. Gennaro ignores the troublemakers and gives Teresina a ring and then they set sail out into the bay in order to be alone.

They are overtaken by a storm and, in spite of help from the other fishermen, Teresina is swept to sea while Gennaro is brought back to the shore. Teresina's mother is mad with worry and accuses Gennaro of carelessness. The other townspeople agree and Gennaro is left alone, almost an outcast. He prays for assistance and the monk tells him that he should go out in search of Teresina and gives him an image of the Madonna to help him.

Far out in the bay, in the Blue Grotto, Golfo, a sea sprite, has his kingdom. He rules over a world of naiads and tritons, fabulous sea beings. Two naiads find the unconscious Teresina, still clutching the guitar she was playing when her little boat was overtaken by the storm. When she wakes she asks Golfo if she can leave for her home, but he is so taken with her beauty that he wants her to stay. He magically changes her into a naiad and she joins the others in their watery dance.

Gennaro discovers the entrance to the Blue Grotto and as he enters, Golfo tries to destroy him with falling rocks. He is not successful and Gennaro is able to go in. He sees the guitar and knows that Teresina must be near. When he sees Golfo he is not afraid of him, but asks where Teresina is. She is brought before him but does not recognize him. Gennaro tries to revive her memory by playing the guitar, but this is no use against the power of Golfo. Then he remembers the Madonna and prays that Teresina will recognize him. She does and the two lovers are united. Golfo is very angry and tries to stop them returning to the mainland. He commands a storm and huge waves beat around the grotto. But Teresina's belief in the Madonna is stronger than Golfo's powers and he is forced to let them go. He does so with good grace, giving them a marvellous treasure from the watery depths.

While the villagers are at a religious festival Teresina suddenly appears, though they thought her lost for ever. She tells them how Gennaro saved her, but the superstitious people do not believe it possible. They think that witchcraft must have been involved. Fortunately the monk is able to convince them that it was the power of the Madonna, which he gave to Gennaro, that caused this miracle.

The crowd dance in celebration with the young people showing off their most brilliant steps. The festivities end with a lively tarantella for all, while Teresina and Gennaro are lifted into an decorated cart and pulled back to the town for their wedding.

Coppélia

This ballet was created in the years which followed the Romantic age, when audiences began to tire of supernatural stories. It is typical of the type of ballet which uses real people in real situations, as well as those which introduce character dances from many countries, in this case the czardas and mazurka.

Coppélia was one of the last great ballets to be created in France as by this time, 1870, the great Petipa was already working in Russia. Ballet in France would soon become more famous for giving the audience an excuse to see pretty ballerinas rather than great ballet.

The story of *Coppélia* is taken from one by E. T. A. Hoffmann (*The Tales of Hoffmann*) and the choreography was by Arthur Saint-Léon. It is very difficult to say how much of the original choreography you are now likely to see, perhaps just some of the mime in the first act and the doll dances in the second act. You will find that different productions, such as those for London Festival Ballet and the New York City Ballet, have very different steps for the village celebrations in the third act. The story, however, is nearly always the same, no matter what the setting.

Coppélia is the name of the mysterious girl who sits reading in the window of the house of the inventor, Dr Coppélius. Swanilda lives in the same village and, in spite of all her efforts, she cannot catch the attention of Coppélia. Swanilda's boyfriend, Franz, is also very interested in Coppélia, so much so that Swanilda is very jealous.

When Swanilda and Franz meet in the village square, he tells her that he truly loves her. She is not impressed, especially after he kills the butterfly she has just caught. If he can behave so cruelly to the pretty thing she treasured, he might be just as heartless with her. Her mind is taken off these problems by the arrival of a group of gypsies who dance a lively mazurka. They are followed by the village mayor who announces that there is to be a celebration in the square to mark the gift of a new bell for their church. To add to the occasion the local lord has also proposed to give handsome presents to the village newlyweds.

When Swanilda is asked if she is to be wed, she cannot answer, as she is now not sure of Franz's true intentions. To try to predict the future, she uses an ear of corn. If it makes a noise when shaken, he will love her; if it is quiet and the seeds inside are shrivelled and dead, he does not. She chooses an ear and shakes it. She can hear nothing. Franz can hear nothing either and, although her friends try to convince her that she is wrong, she is now quite sure that she will not marry. Her sadness is overshadowed by the czardas which her friends dance. Tired of all this activity, the crowd leave as night falls.

When the square is empty, Dr Coppélius comes out of his house. He locks the door very carefully, to protect his inventions, and wraps the key in his big handkerchief before putting it in his pocket. As he goes on his way to the inn for his evening drink, he is set upon by the village lads who tease him and twirl him around. When they run off laughing he is left hot and bothered. He takes his handkerchief out and mops his brow before setting on his way again. He does not see or hear the key dropping to the ground.

Swanilda and her friends see the key and decide that at last they will find out who the mysterious girl is. They creep into the house, knees quivering as they go. Just as they are going in through the front door, Franz creeps below the window with a ladder. He too is determined to find out once and for all why he gets no response from the girl in the window. As he is halfway up the ladder Dr Coppélius comes back into the square searching for his key. He chases Franz away and then notices that his door is open. He creeps in to see who has gained entry. As he does so, the persistent Franz tries once more to climb in through the window.

Inside the house Swanilda and her friends find a large dark room full of curious figures sitting on different chairs and pedestals. They look so human that the girls are afraid at first. They jump with fright when one girl accidentally presses against a doll and it bursts into action. After a moment of complete panic they realize that the figures are all just mechanical dolls.

Swanilda looks into the window alcove for the girl and wheels her into the room. They find out that she is just a mechanical doll as well, but a doll with almost human features. As the girls play with the dolls Dr Coppélius creeps in quietly and then chases them out. The girls flee, all except Swanilda who hides with Coppélia behind the window curtain.

When things quieten down a little Dr Coppélius starts to tidy up, but sees Franz climbing in through the window. He takes him by surprise,

---

Jack Carter's production of *Coppélia* for London Festival Ballet: Dagmar Kessler (Swanilda) is supported by Alain Dubreuil (Franz) while she shakes the ear of corn to find out if he truly loves her.

but instead of being angry and throwing him out, he offers him a drink. Franz does not notice that Dr Coppélius has put a potion in the drink and accepts more glassfuls. He does not know that the Doctor has a plan to try to give his beloved Coppélia, the greatest of his creations, real life. He now plans to use his old spells, taken from dusty books, to move the life force from the sleeping Franz to Coppélia.

When Franz is completely unconscious Dr Coppélius consults his books and then wheels Coppélia from her alcove. As he reads the books the doll appears to come alive of its own free will, but it is really Swanilda in the doll's clothes. She was horrified when she guessed the Doctor's plan and has decided to trick him. As he waves his hands over her, trying to give her life, she throws away the book she is reading. Doctor Coppélius believes his plan is working. She then moves her arms and her head and sits and stands. Her face still does not move until Coppélius tries another spell. First the eyelashes flutter and then feeling comes to the whole body. He is overjoyed as she appears to become more human with each wave of his hand. He tries to make her dance, first a Spanish and then a Scottish dance. Swanilda makes her movements wilder and wilder, as she is really looking for a way to free Franz from the Doctor's clutches. She upsets piles of books and tries to rouse Franz. As the Doctor wheels her back to her alcove, Franz wakes up, not knowing what has happened. Swanilda changes back into her own clothes and bursts back into the room. She runs about, setting all the dolls in action and then rushes out with Franz. Poor Doctor Coppélius is completely muddled. He goes to the window to find his beloved Coppélia only to discover a lifeless doll lying naked across the chair.

The following day the Festival of the Bells takes place in the village square and presents are given to those about to wed. Swanilda and Franz have now been reunited after an adventure which proved that they really loved each other. Dr Coppélius arrives and makes a great scene complaining about the damage caused by the young people. Swanilda is very sad as she understands how lonely and unhappy he must have been to hope that his doll would come to life. She offers him her present from the lord which he accepts. The mayor, however, insists he give it back and he makes a special award to the Doctor. Everyone is satisfied and they wait for the pageant, danced by the villagers, to begin.

The pageant shows the passing of the hours and starts with the Dance of the Hours. Dawn is shown in a simple dance for a young girl while Prayer is a sombre dance for a nun-like figure. Then there are dances showing Work, War and Peace. Franz leads in the warriors, while Swanilda is the figure of Peace. Together they end the performance.

The Sleeping Beauty

This was the first of the great classic ballets which Marius Petipa created in St Petersburg, now known as Leningrad, for the Tsar and his court in 1890. It is an important ballet, not only for the steps and the wonderful dances which Petipa created, but also for the way the story was told and the décor created. It was the vision of one man—Vsevolozhsky, the director of the Imperial Theatres—and he supervised each detail. Last, but not least, Tchaikovsky wrote another great score which has given countless millions of people great enjoyment ever since. It is very hard to believe that this wonderful story, taken from the fairy story by Perrault, was not received very well when it was first performed.

At the celebrations for the christening of King Florestan's baby daughter, the Princess Aurora, the fairies led by the Lilac Fairy come to bestow gifts upon the baby. Unfortunately, the court chamberlain did not invite the fairy Carabosse. Halfway through the proceedings she arrives in a terrible rage, surrounded by ugly creatures. She tears the hair from the unfortunate chamberlain and then puts a curse on the baby. She predicts that when the baby Princess becomes sixteen she will prick her finger on a spindle and die. The court is horrified, but the Lilac Fairy, the symbol of goodness, has not yet given her gift. She cannot undo the evil spell, but she is able to weaken it. Aurora will not die, she will sleep for one hundred years and be woken by the kiss of a handsome prince.

Sixteen years pass and it is Aurora's coming of age. She has grown into the most beautiful Princess and four princes from each corner of the world have come to ask for her hand in marriage.

Throughout the kingdom precautions have been taken to protect Aurora. Pins, needles and spindles have been banned. It is only through the kindness of the Queen that four old ladies have been pardoned following a death sentence for owning knitting needles.

Aurora comes into the rose garden to meet the princes and dances with joy. Her mother introduces her to them and she dances with them, each supporting her in a brilliant balance. When the dance ends and she has collected roses from the princes an old lady comes forward and offers her a posy of flowers. Aurora accepts and runs to show it to her mother. As she does so, she cries with pain and looks at her finger. The posy is thrown to the ground where it breaks apart to reveal a spindle inside. The old lady throws off her cloak to show that she is really Carabosse.

Aurora dances deliriously from group to group, showing the courtiers the wound on her finger before falling to the ground at her mother's feet. The court cluster around while Carabosse sweeps off triumphantly.

In their moment of panic the King and Queen have forgotten the gift

Anneli Alhanko and Per-Arthur Segerström in the controversial production of *The Sleeping Beauty* which Ulf Gadd produced for the Royal Swedish Ballet.

of the Lilac Fairy, who now appears to remind them that Aurora is not dead, but will sleep for a hundred years. Aurora is carried to a flower-strewn bed and as she lies there the court fall into a deep sleep and the Lilac Fairy magically causes a thick forest of thorny trees to grow around the castle.

A hundred years later the Prince Florimund is out hunting with a large party of courtiers, including his fiancée. He feels that there is something special about this part of the forest and even the games and dances of his courtiers cannot distract him. Finally he sends the party on its way as he wishes to spend a few quiet moments alone. The Lilac Fairy appears and tells him about the beautiful Princess who lies asleep deep in the forest. He immediately knows that this is what he has been dreaming about for many years. The Lilac Fairy produces a vision of Aurora before him and they dance, but she is soon spirited away. He begs the Lilac Fairy to take him to her through the thorny forest. The way is difficult and he is attacked by Carabosse and her fierce attendants, but he cuts his way through until he reaches the place where Aurora lies. He is taken with her beauty and kisses her.

Aurora slowly wakes and gazes into his eyes. Slowly the whole court comes to life and Florimund asks the King for Aurora's hand in marriage. He gladly consents.

At the grand wedding party for Aurora and Florimund the Lilac Fairy brings fairy-tale characters to entertain the court. They marvel at the White Cat, Puss in Boots, Bluebeard and his wife and the enchanted Princess with the Bluebird of happiness. Finally Aurora and her Prince dance together to show their undying love before they join the last grand mazurka for the whole court.

The Nutcracker

This is perhaps the most popular ballet and the one which you are almost certain to have a chance to see. Almost every company in the world, large or small, perform it, usually at Christmas time. This tradition arises out of the story, as it was not created as a Christmas ballet.

After the moderate success of *The Sleeping Beauty* with the Tsar, and its growing popularity with audiences, Tchaikovsky was asked to write more ballet music. He wasn't very happy with it, but it has turned out to be one of his most glorious scores.

Although the ballet is less than a century old (first performed in 1892), the original choreography of much of it has been lost and nearly every production seen today has different choreography. Only the *Grand pas de deux* will have some of the original steps. Even the story will differ greatly and it has been retold so many ways that occasionally it is unrecognizable. Here is the basic story from which all the variations come.

At a Christmas party in the home of Herr Stahlbaum, an important merchant, the most intriguing guest is Dr Drosselmeyer who has brought some unusual presents for Clara and Fritz, the Stahlbaum children. He shows them dancing dolls and gives Clara a pair of dancing shoes and a nutcracker in the shape of a toy soldier.

After the excitement of the party with its dancing and rich food, Clara cannot sleep and returns to the drawing room to find her Nutcracker doll below the large Christmas tree. As she approaches it the figure of Dr Drosselmeyer appears from behind the tree. With a wave of his cloaked arms he makes the tree grow. Across the darkened room scamper big mice which frighten Clara, but an army of toy soldiers, led by her Nutcracker, march out and engage them in battle. The soldiers bring on a big cannon to help them, but the mice manage to take it away. The evil Mouse-King leads his forces and it looks as though they are going to win.

As the battle draws near its close the Mouse-King knocks over the Nutcracker and almost kills him. At exactly the right moment Clara throws her dance shoe at the Mouse-King. He is distracted and the Nutcracker is able to take the advantage and kill him.

As thanks for saving his life the Nutcracker, now transformed into a handsome prince, takes Clara on a fabulous journey. The Christmas tree grows even bigger and is changed into a tall fir tree at the centre of a beautiful snowy landscape. Snowflakes dance in fluttering patterns, led by the Snow Queen. She dances with the Prince to entertain Clara, before they set out on the next part of their journey: to the Land of Sweets. Clara rides on a walnut boat until they reach the colourful City of Sweets where the walls are marzipan and the columns candy. They are met by the Sugar Plum Fairy and her cavaliers. The Prince tells how Clara saved his life in the great battle with the mice and the Sugar Plum Fairy orders a feast of sweets as a reward. Each course is attended by a suitable dance. Arabs dance with the coffee; busy Chinese with the tea. Pretty marzipan shepherdesses twirl before a great host of flowers swirl on for a grand waltz. Finally the Sugar Plum Fairy and the Prince dance a very grand duet.

Clara again feels tired and waves goodbye to the sweets, the Sugar Plum Fairy and the Prince. As they fade away she sinks into sleep.

While Clara has been away on this wonderful journey her parents have noticed that she is not in her bed. They search the house for her and find her curled up beneath the Christmas tree with her Nutcracker doll safely in her arms. On her face there is a very happy, contented look.

Swan Lake

This is the third of the ballets you will know of as classics. They are called this not just because they are the standard works by which we now measure all others, but also because of the pure classical style of dance which Petipa created for them.

Really this was the first great ballet which Tchaikovsky wrote. Unfortunately the first production was made by someone else, not Petipa, in 1877, and it was not a success. In fact it was a terrible failure and after a few performances in Moscow it gradually faded away.

Tchaikovsky never knew of the eventual success of his ballet as it was

---

The Nutcracker changes very much from production to production and includes different dances for the *divertissements* in the Land of Sweets. In the old London Festival Ballet production Michael Ho, now a talented modern dancer, performed a brilliant jig.

Merle Park and Anthony Dowell as Odette and Siegfried in *Swan Lake*.

not until after his death that the music was used again. *The Sleeping Beauty* and *The Nutcracker* had had some success, so after Tchaikovsky's death Lev Ivanov, who had worked with Petipa and had created the choreography for the Sugar Plum Fairy, had the idea of reviving just the second act at a memorial concert for Tchaikovsky. The following season the whole ballet was presented and it has become perhaps the most popular ballet ever. The picture of a Swan is almost everyone's idea of

ballet, but beware! Many people think that the Dying Swan, that beautiful solo to music by Saint-Säens, comes from *Swan Lake*, but that was created over ten years later for Anna Pavlova.

There are many versions of the classic ballets, some almost unrecognizable when you read the original story. In the Scottish Ballet version Prince Siegfried only sees Odette while under the influence of drugs, while in Hamburg the whole scene beside the lake is a court entertainment for the mad King Ludwig of Bavaria! The New York City Ballet only perform the second act, but George Balanchine has inserted a solo for the Prince.

During the celebrations of Prince Siegfried's coming of age the courtiers and peasants bring gifts and dance for him. His mother brings her gift: a jewelled crossbow. She also announces that he must now choose a bride and that a great ball with be held in the palace, when all the eligible princesses from far and wide will be presented to him. At first Siegfried refuses, but when he sees that his mother is angry he pretends to agree. He is more interested in his new crossbow. While he is thinking about his problem a flight of swans pass overhead and he decides that he will go to the forest to shoot them. He tells his tutor to gather together the huntsmen and they go off into the forest.

In the forest they reach a lake on which the flight of swans have landed. They seem to be led by one swan, bigger and more beautiful than the rest. In the distance it looks as though a small jewelled crown is glittering on its head. The huntsmen are excited and call Siegfried to see the swans. He is fascinated by the sight, but feels that there is something magical in the air. These cannot be ordinary swans. He sends the huntsmen into the forest to search further while he remains alone with his unhappiness. He hears a sound and hides. Into the glade comes a beautiful creature who appears to be part woman, part swan. Siegfried approaches her, but she is surprised and tries to flutter away. Siegfried begs her not to fly away from him and asks who she is. He has already been captured by her beauty and to reassure her he lays aside his crossbow. She tells him that she is Odette and that the evil magician Von Rothbart has transformed her from a beautiful princess into a swan and that the lake they are beside is made from her mother's tears. She is allowed to take earthly form only during the hours of darkness and during the day must become a swan once more. She can only be released from this terrible fate by someone who swears to love her and no one else. Siegfried immediately swears eternal love, but he is interrupted by the arrival of Von Rothbart who claims Odette back into his power. Siegfried attempts to kill him, but Odette warns that this would not release her, but commit her to being a swan for ever. Arm in arm they go into the forest together.

The glade is soon filled by the other swan maidens in Von Rothbart's power and Siegfried's huntsmen find them. At first they are amazed, but then they try to shoot them. Siegfried arrives in time to stop them as Odette begs for mercy.

When the huntsmen go back into the forest on Siegfried's orders, the swan maidens dance for him in large sweeping movements; the big swans crossing the glade with beautiful arm movements just like wings, while the little swans dance with small, fast steps. Odette and Siegfried then dance a tender duet to show their devotion.

As dawn approaches Odette and the swan maidens are once more drawn to the lake. As the maidens become swans again Siegfried tries to keep Odette with him, but the power of Von Rothbart is so great that her beautiful soft movements become stiff and rigid as she too becomes a swan. Siegfried is left alone, but he is determined to find her and marry her. He will keep his vow.

The following evening the great ball takes place. Siegfried is moody and sullen, much to his mother's annoyance. He is ungracious to the beautiful princesses who are presented to him and will not make a choice. The princesses have been accompanied by ambassadors and entertainers from their home countries. They now dance to entertain the court. During the entertainment a fanfare announces an unexpected guest; a tall knight with his beautiful daughter dressed in glittering black. She looks exactly like Odette and Siegfried is sure that it is her. He seizes her hand and together they leave the ballroom. The entertainment continues with a Polish mazurka and a lively tarantella, before Siegfried runs back into the room and tells his mother that the mysterious visitor is Odette and that he will marry her. He dances a brilliant duet with Odette, who is really Odile, the daughter of Von Rothbart. Siegfried is almost hypnotized by her glamour and cannot see that Von Rothbart is telling her how to charm him. So overcome is he with her beauty that he does not see the helpless Odette fluttering outside one of the tall ballroom windows. At the end of their dance he asks Von Rothbart if he may marry his daughter. Von Rothbart agrees, but asks Siegfried to swear eternal love for her. Siegfried, thinking he is making his vow stronger and not breaking it, happily does so. Von Rothbart now knows he has won and he and Odile rush out of the ballroom triumphantly, leaving the court in disarray. Siegfried does not know what to do. As his mother faints in the confusion, he runs from the palace in a frantic search for Odette.

The swan maidens are gathered at the lakeside full of foreboding for the fate of their queen. She returns weeping and tells them that she has been betrayed through Von Rothbart's trickery and must now remain a swan for ever. She would prefer to die than to live as a swan and tries to throw herself in the lake. The swan maidens stop her and cluster around her for comfort.

As a storm breaks Siegfried reaches the lakeside and looks for Odette amongst the swans. When he finds her he begs her forgiveness and takes her in his arms. After a tender duet she tells him that it does not matter that he was tricked. The vow was broken and there is no way that she can take earthly form again. Her life is now in Von Rothbart's hands for ever. She tells Siegfried that only death can now release her from Von Rothbart's power, however hard Siegfried fights him. Odette throws herself into the lake. Siegfried is so much in love with her that he must be with her in death as in life. He throws himself into the lake after her. This demonstration of true love brings Von Rothbart's downfall and the swan maidens destroy him. Though Odette and Siegfried could not love on earth they are joined forever in eternity.

Les Sylphides

This is the first ballet we have come across which does not have a definite story, other than the various *divertissements* which appear in the classic ballets. Those were dancing to show off steps. This has a definite mood, but at the end it is up to you to decide what may or may not have happened!

A poet is seen in the woods, dreaming, surrounded by the Sylphides who represent creatures of his imagination. Why he is in the wood or where the wood is we do not know and it does not matter.

This ballet was created in 1909 by Mikhail Fokine to music by Chopin, for the earliest seasons of Diaghilev's company and is very similar to the 'white' acts of both *La Sylphide* and *Giselle* from the Romantic period. They are usually called *ballets blancs*.

The scene is a woodland clearing with an old, ruined church in the distance. The Sylphides are found standing, quite still, around the glade. In the centre, wearing a black velvet tunic with a big white bow, stands the Poet, surrounded by the three main Sylphides.

As the music grows the group of Sylphides slowly unfold from their pose and vanish into the woods. The Poet is inspired by the Sylphides who dance for him, first a waltz, then a mazurka and a beautiful Prelude. He dances a waltz with one of them before all the Sylphides enter for a big waltz. Halfway through this the Poet stops dancing as though wondering where he is. He returns to the place he was standing at the beginning and is joined by the Sylphides resting at his side and in front of him.

Was it all a dream brought about by the beautiful natural scenery?

A backstage view of *Les Sylphides*.

The Firebird

Serge Diaghilev was not a dancer, choreographer, designer, or musician. His special genius was to bring together all these people to make beautiful ballets. He felt very strongly that every part of a ballet should fit perfectly together and not be just a collection of dances performed in front of a pretty backcloth. He also brought out of Russia the first ballets which used old Russian stories, which, in 1909, made a very great impact.

The Firebird is taken from old Russian folk tales and was first shown in Paris in 1910. It is important not just for the dancing (the first Firebird was Tamara Karsavina who worked afterwards for many years in London) but also for the glowing décor and the wonderful rich music by Igor Stravinsky. This was the first of the many great pieces of ballet music he would write.

Below
The coronation ceremony, with David Drew as Ivan and Vergie Derman as the Princess.

Opposite
The Firebird (Alfreda Thorogood) with the enchanted Princesses.

A high wall guards the enchanted garden of the evil magician Katschei. It protects the trees with their golden apples and prevents the escape of the beautiful captive princesses.

The Firebird appears and tries to take the golden fruit from the trees, but she has been followed by Prince Ivan who tries to capture her. He succeeds, but agrees to set her free after she has given him one of her magic feathers. This will protect him if he should be caught by Katschei as he explores the garden.

Prince Ivan watches as the princesses pass their lonely days playing with the golden apples. As they throw them to each other, he approaches them. He speaks with the most beautiful and together they dance for the others. The princesses appear happy with the intruder until they hear Katschei calling. Ivan is left alone, but he determines to rescue the princesses. As he waits in the garden he is soon surrounded by Katschei's fabulous monsters. Soon the magician himself comes and threatens to turn Ivan into stone in spite of pleas by the princess. But Ivan does not appear to be afraid. He remembers the magic feather which the Firebird gave him. He produces it and the Firebird appears to help him. She makes the monsters dance violently until they collapse and she tells Ivan that the soul of the magician lies in a great egg inside the cave. Ivan runs into the cave and brings out the egg. He smashes it to the ground where it shatters into many pieces. As it breaks Katschei falls down dead and his spell is broken. The princesses are free and Ivan claims the most beautiful as his bride.

Amongst scenes of great splendour he marries her. As the crowns are placed on their heads long files of nobles and clergy in their most elaborate gowns enter to pay homage.

Petrushka

In many ways this is the best example of how Diaghilev combined story, music, décor and character into a perfect ballet. You cannot separate one from the other. It is like a complete painting. Even when the music is played in a concert hall you will feel the story and want to see the action.

Most of the productions you are likely to see follow the story very closely and many use décor closely modelled on the original by Benois (1911). Of course it is very difficult for every production to be a faithful copy of the original, as the many dancers who took part in that have slightly different recollections of what happened and different scenic artists interpret the décor in different ways. In spite of this all productions are remarkably similar.

It is carnival time in St Petersburg and the people are having a last celebration before Lent which they will observe with a fast. There are fairground booths full of good things to buy, games to play and shows to watch.

In the centre of this snowy scene stands the booth of the Showman who advertises his puppets. Street dancers and acrobats try to attract rival crowds while ribbon sellers tempt people with their wares. There is constant bustle and activity which only stops when two drummers appear to announce that the Showman is going to bring his puppets into action. When a crowd has gathered, he pushes his head through the curtains and then comes out to the front of his booth. He plays a few unusual bars on his flute and the crowd wait to see what will happen.

The curtains part suddenly to show a stage divided into three compartments. In each there is a lifeless puppet supported by armrests. In the middle is the Ballerina with brightly coloured cheeks and a hat perched jauntily on her head. On her right is a Moor with bright eyes peering out of his black face, a gold turban and richly coloured trousers held up by a broad, bright sash. To her left is the limp figure of the clown, Petrushka with his sad pale face.

The Showman finishes his tune and then, with some sharp notes, he commands the puppets to dance. At first they dance, moving only their legs as they dangle on their armrests. Then they dance out into the crowd which moves back in amazement. Slowly it becomes apparent that the three dolls are taking part in a drama of their own. The Moor and Petrushka are both trying to attract the favours of the Ballerina. She appears to like the Moor best which drives Petrushka to a frenzy. He attacks the Moor. The Showman brings the performance to a close when he sees this and sends the dolls back to their compartments where they once more hang lifeless.

However, when the curtains close, the drama continues long after the fair has ended for the day. Petrushka is thrown roughly into this cell by the Showman. As the door is shut he tries to leave, but his efforts are sad and hopeless. He moves around the room, pounding on the walls and door in the hope that someone will hear him, but it is useless. He must lie alone with large portrait of the hated Showman watching over him. He shows his frustration in tortured movements suggesting that he has human feelings although only a puppet.

The Ballerina comes into his room which makes him happy for a moment, but she is just taunting him. All his efforts to attract her attention make her leave. His anger shows by banging at the walls until one breaks. Even now he cannot escape. He just hangs there, lifeless.

The Moor in his brightly coloured room lies lazily surrounded by the exotic designs of palm trees and entwined borders. He plays with a coconut, tossing it in the air and catching it. He does not know what it is and shakes it to hear what is inside. His gestures are stupid as he really is a senseless puppet. He tries to crack the coconut with his sword, but still cannot open it. As his efforts are useless he decides that it must be a magic object and he crouches on his knees to worship it. As he does so the door opens and the Ballerina struts in. She is happily and rather simple-mindedly playing a trumpet. She dances to amuse the Moor who, unlike Petrushka, does not frighten her away. He pulls her to his couch and she does not resist. In fact she seems very content to sit on his lap. While she is there Petrushka pushes his way into the room almost as though he has come to save the Ballerina from the Moor's advances. They do not want to be interrupted and the Moor reaches for his sword. Petrushka escapes in the nick of time and the Moor and Ballerina are left together.

Outside the booth the crowd has gathered for another day of entertainment. The big nursemaids dance with their coloured handkerchiefs and are soon joined by the burly coachmen. As evening draws in, snow

The Moor (Keith Rosson), the Ballerina (Nadia Nerina) and Petrushka (Rudolf Nureyev) in the Royal Ballet production of *Petrushka*.

begins to fall. Wildly dressed characters, some with enormous animal masks on, as well as demons and devils join in the festivities. As the crowd swirl around, there is a sudden commotion behind the curtain of the Showman's booth. The crowd stop moving and stand aside as the commotion becomes more violent and the curtain shakes. It is thrown aside and Petrushka comes running out trying to escape from the mad Moor who is brandishing his sword. Petrushka falls to the ground and covers his head, but it is not enough to ward off the vicious blow. After a few violent shivers he topples over, dead.

The crowd push around the body for they were quite sure that he was

real and a murder has been committed. Some run to bring in the guards who ask the Showman what has happened. Shrugging his shoulders he tells them all not to worry. It was only play-acting by his puppets. The crowd insist it was murder, but the Showman pushes them aside and picks up the limp bedraggled body. He shakes the lifeless puppet in the air. The crowd cannot understand it, but they have to believe the Showman. As night falls they drift away, leaving the Showman alone in front of his booth. As he turns to walk away he is horrified to see the ghost of Petrushka high above the roof, shaking his fist in a last defiant gesture.

Afternoon of a Faun

When this ballet was first danced in 1912 it caused a great scandal. Some members of the audience did not like the way the story was told and nearly all disliked the very peculiar steps Vaslav Nijinsky invented. He had been a brilliant classical dancer himself, so the audience expected wonderful leaps and turns. Instead Nijinsky chose to make new movements, based on poses taken from Greek wall paintings and the decorations on pottery. This meant that the dancers hardly danced at all. They walked in a very odd way, always with their sides to the audience, as though pressed against a flat background. You can still sometimes see this ballet performed today, but you are more likely to see a modern version created by Jerome Robbins.

Nijinsky had the vision of a faun, half man, half animal, lying on a grassy bank in the summer heat. He is playing the flute and lazily eating grapes. A group of nymphs dressed in filmy clothes have been bathing nearby. They pass the faun in a line with linked arms. He is intrigued by them and comes down from his resting place. The nymphs are just as interested in this strange creature. As he moves about them, they become frightened and leave. However their interest is so great that they timidly return, only to be frightened away again. Their leader is not so afraid and becomes attached to the faun. They touch briefly, but she is very playful and tries to keep out of his grasp. Soon she feels that she must join her sisters and runs into the woods, leaving behind a silken scarf. This is the only memento the faun has of his brief meeting with the beautiful nymphs and he takes it to his resting place where he lies caressing it to bring back his daydream.

Antoinette Sibley and Anthony Dowell in the Royal Ballet production of *Afternoon of a Faun*.

Jerome Robbins took the idea of the Nijinsky ballet and turned it into a story of today. It is set in a ballet studio with one wall of mirrors. It is through this 'wall' that we watch the action. We are the mirror that the dancers are reflected in.

A boy lies asleep on the studio floor. As the music grows he stirs, waking slowly, stretching and arching his back and muscles. He sits up and stares at himself in the mirror, posing to admire his own body. He appears to fall back to sleep. As he does a girl in ballet practice clothes tiptoes into the studio. As she enters she looks only at her own image in the mirror. As she begins to exercise, the boy wakes and watches her reflection in the mirror. As she moves to the centre of the studio, he rises to support her, never looking directly at her. The beautiful poses they make are only admired through reflection. They end their brief duet kneeling in front of the mirror. They kiss lightly. As the boy's hand moves to her cheek she stands and, still looking only at the mirror, steps slowly backwards out of the room.

The boy watches her image fade away and, with a few more stretching movements to admire himself, he falls again into a deep sleep.

La Boutique Fantasque

When Nijinsky left the Diaghilev company after his marriage, Massine took his place as both dancer and choreographer. In his years with the company he created many works which are still often performed today. Of these the story of the fantastic toyshop, first performed in 1919, is perhaps the most popular.

In the best toyshop in the south of France the owner makes the most wonderful dolls. They are in great demand by the many visitors who come on holiday from all over the world.

When the shop opens there are already many customers waiting to choose the best of the dolls. The English visitors and an American family watch very realistic peasant dancers and two brilliant tarantella dancers perform. A Russian family arrives and more dolls, including a snob, a melon seller and two poodles, show off their tricks.

The shopkeeper chooses this moment to produce the two best dolls he has ever made, the can-can dancers. After they perform their brilliant dance both the American and the Russian families want to buy them. To try to please both, the shopkeeper allows each family to have one doll.

When the shop is closed for the night and the shopkeeper and his assistant leave, locking the doors safely behind them, the dolls come out from their boxes. It is an evening of great drama as they are all concerned that the two can-can dancers are to be separated and sent to the opposite sides of the world. They dance together happily, although they know that this may be the last time they are able to do so. In the end they decide that they cannot bear to be parted and, with the help of the other dolls, run away together.

When the shop opens in the morning the Russian and American families come early to collect their parcels. They check the boxes to see if they have the correct dolls, but find both empty. The families are furious with the shopkeeper and the ill-mannered children chase him round the shop to show how disappointed they are. The whole shop is upset by the irate customers, but the other dolls decide to come to the rescue. The families are chased from the shop and are left to peer in through the windows as the dolls inside dance to celebrate the fact that the two lovers are still together.

Serenade

Just as Massine and others found work in Europe, so George Balanchine went to America soon after the death of Diaghilev. There he founded a school, the School of American Ballet, which still produces wonderful dancers today. For his students he created a ballet to fit their talents. That ballet is *Serenade* (1934) and although created for students it is now given wonderful performances by major companies ranging from the Royal Ballet in Britain to the Dutch National Ballet. It is really the first American classical ballet and now finds its place in the repertoires of many of the companies scattered across America. Set to Tchaikovsky's *Serenade for Strings* it has a theme, like *Les Sylphides*, but no story. It is full of incidents, but they are not related to a particular story. They simply suggest emotions to you; if a girl falls to the ground you may feel sad that she appears dead, if a girl is carried off high above the other dancers' heads you may feel elated.

The ballet opens after a few strong chords to show the stage full of girls, evenly spaced out with their feet together, toes pointed forward. They wear long soft skirts. As they respond to the music they turn out their feet in the distinctive ballet way. The girls then dance increasingly faster and faster, suddenly returning to the opening motionless tableau. One girl arrives late to take her place in the group. A boy enters and walks towards the girl and as he does so the others leave the stage.

This couple then perform a sweeping waltz and are soon joined by the other girls. The ballerina dances in and out of them before rejoining her

Serenade by George Balanchine.

partner before the waltz comes to an end. They leave the stage, but five girls remain. They sit on the stage making elegant gestures to each other, almost as though making conversation. As a strong Russian melody appears through the music a boy joins them and dances with one of the girls. As they run from the stage one girl falls and lies on the floor.

From one corner another girl enters, walking behind another boy, her hand over his eyes. She guides him to the girl on the floor. He helps her from the ground and dances with her as well as with the girl who led him

in. At last he must choose between them. He leaves with the girl he came in with. The other girl again falls to the floor, this time for ever. The other girls come in and carry her off the stage high above their heads as she slowly arches her back and opens her arms in a last eloquent appeal.

Gaité Parisienne

When the Diaghilev company had to disband, following his death in 1929, many very talented people had to find work elsewhere. Massine worked with different companies which tried to carry on the name of the Russian ballet and for them he made many popular and lasting ballets, including *Gaité Parisienne* in 1938.

Gaité Parisienne is the story of one evening in a Paris nightclub towards the end of the last century. The staff are getting the gorgeous room ready for opening. Waiters polish tables and cleaning girls scrub the floors.

The Flower Girl, who will go from table to table with her posies, arrives. She gives each waiter a little bouquet and in return they give her a drink with which she toasts their health. Three hostesses arrive with their escorts, soon to be followed by the Glove Seller. She dances with the escorts who are attracted by her quiet beauty which is in contrast to the more lively characters of either the hostesses or the Flower Girl.

While they are dancing a rich Peruvian, new to town and eager to spend, arrives. He still has his bags in his hand, so keen is he to sample Paris night life. He buys a buttonhole from the Flower Girl and then, noticing the Glove Seller, tries on some of her wares. He is so excited by the prospect of a evening's fun that he can never stop dancing, even while trying on the gloves.

Business begins to get more brisk and a handsome Baron enters. The waiters gather round to take his cloak knowing that there will be a good tip and the Flower Seller tries to interest him in her blossoms. It is the Glove Seller who attracts him most and, ignoring everyone else, he asks her to dance with him. Meanwhile the Peruvian orders champagne for the hostesses, but loses them to some handsome soldiers who come in. Everyone is looking for a partner that evening and though the Baron is infatuated with the Glove Seller, he cannot take his eyes off a fashionable beauty. For a little while the Baron leaves the Glove Seller and she spends a moment with the Peruvian who is still buying champagne and perfume. The Baron is furious at this and becomes involved in a fight between the various rivals for the attentions of the ladies. The fight spills out into the street while the Peruvian, mystified by this odd behaviour, hides under a table.

The Baron is finally reunited with the Glove Seller who has assured him that she was only being kind to the Peruvian. As they dance the night-club comes back to life and the can-can dancers, led by their high-kicking master, dance for the crowd. Even the Peruvian, now complete with top hat, joins in.

As the night draws on the various couples leave. Each lady has found the gentleman of her choice. The Glove Seller and the Baron are the last to leave—except for the Peruvian. He has seen much happen, but has been left alone at the end. He is not at all happy about it.

Romeo and Juliet

This is the story of *Romeo and Juliet* as seen through the eyes of the choreographer Kenneth MacMillan. For the ballet stage the Shakespeare story is simplified and some of the lesser characters and scenes are left out so that we can concentrate on the drama of the two young lovers. There have been many versions of this story, either as full-length, very big productions, such as the famous 1940 Russian one which was made for Galina Ulanova and was first brought to the West by the Bolshoi in 1956. There is also a version by John Cranko (1962), which is very widely performed, in Australia and Canada for instance, and one by Maurice Béjart.

MacMillan and Cranko use the very grand music by Prokofiev that was used by the Bolshoi, and there have been several short versions using the Tchaikovsky Fantasy Overture.

The action takes place in Verona, home of the Montagues and Capulets. Romeo is in love with the Lady Rosaline, who ignores him. His friends Mercutio and Benvolio try to cheer him up as the market place gets busier during the day. Their high spirits lead them into a fight with Tybalt, a nephew of Lord Capulet. The two families have been sworn enemies for many years. Even the two aged Lords join in the fight in a very undignified way. It is only the arrival of the Prince of Verona and his firm commands which brings the fight to an end.

In the Capulet house the young Juliet is playing with her nurse when her parents arrive. Lord and Lady Capulet bring with them a rich young nobleman, Paris, who wishes to marry her. Juliet realizes that she is at last grown up and no longer a child.

The Capulets give a very grand ball to which the guests arrive richly dressed and masked. Romeo, Mercutio and Benvolio decide to follow the Lady Rosaline into the ball. They, too, wear masks.

As the many guests perform the stately dances Romeo and his friends slip in. Juliet is allowed to attend the ball and dances for the guests. Mercutio notices that Romeo has seen Juliet and realizes that he is now in love with this beautiful young girl. He knows this will lead to trouble and tries to distract him. Tybalt sees that Romeo is at the ball and tries to order him out. However, Lord Capulet invites him to stay, and when the ball ends he stops Tybalt chasing after Romeo.

Long after the ball Juliet still cannot sleep and comes out onto her

---

Overleaf
Marcia Haydée and Richard Cragun in John Cranko's *Romeo and Juliet*.

balcony thinking of Romeo. He appears in the garden below. Not considering the risks she rushes down to him and they declare their love for each other.

For days afterwards Romeo can think of no one but Juliet and the wedding processions which pass through the market square make him think of the day he will marry her. While he wastes time there with his friends, Juliet's nurse pushes through the bustling crowd to give him a letter. In it Juliet agrees to marry him.

Romeo and Juliet arrange to meet at the chapel of Friar Laurence who marries them. They believe that their marriage will end the troubles between the two great houses. After the brief ceremony they separate and Romeo returns to find his friends in the market place. As usual trouble breaks out between the two families and Tybalt kills Mercutio. Romeo in a moment of anger takes his revenge and kills Tybalt in return. The Prince arrives on the scene and exiles him from the city. He spends a last night with Juliet before leaving the city.

Juliet wakes up alone to be greeted by her parents and Paris. She refuses to marry him and he storms out. Her father is furious and threatens to disown her. They leave her in her room alone. She decides that she must go to seek the advice of Friar Laurence.

After Juliet has begged for his help, he agrees and gives her a potion. This will make her fall into a sleep which her parents will think is the sleep of death. They will bury her in the family tomb. Friar Laurence will warn Romeo of the plan so that he can be ready to carry her away from the tomb and the city.

To satisfy her parents Juliet agrees to marry Paris, but then takes the potion. The next morning her friends arrive with her beautiful wedding dress only to find her lying on her bed, apparently dead.

By an unfortunate mischance Romeo does not receive Friar Laurence's message and comes back to Verona after hearing of the death of Juliet. He believes the news is true and makes his way to the huge family tomb to find his beloved Juliet.

He is so shocked by the sight of her that he does not know what to do. He finds Paris near her body and kills him. He then kills himself by poison believing that he can never be with her again.

Juliet slowly wakes from the drugged sleep to find Romeo dead beside her. Taking the dagger with which he killed Paris she stabs herself.

Spartacus

This is a very grand-scale ballet danced by the Bolshoi Ballet of Moscow. In this form it has not been danced by a company in the West, but several have attempted different versions.

Even the Russian version had its problems before the company arrived at the very successful version that they now dance. The idea of a ballet based on the slaves rising up against the power of Rome (also the subject of an epic film which you may have seen) had been around for some time. In fact there were several attempts at the ballet in the nineteen-fifties and early 'sixties. Although they used the same music by Khatchaturian (which sounds a little as though it came from a film) the scale of the story defeated them.

Then in 1968 Yuri Grigorovich attempted his production and he devised a very clever way of dividing up the scenes. He separated the large-scale crowd scenes, when the massed Roman legions or the hordes of slaves cross the stage, from the scenes which tell the story. It was almost like a film with cinemascope effects and then close-ups.

This ballet is perfect for the athletic style of the Bolshoi, but few other companies, if any, could put onto the stage such a large male *corps de ballet* all of whom looked heroic in size.

The four leading parts have been danced by all the great Bolshoi dancers of recent years, in particular Maris Liepa, Mikhail Lavrovsky, Vladimir Vasiliev, Natalia Bessmertnova and Ekaterina Maximova.

The Roman Empire is kept firmly under Rome's rule by the power of the legions led by Crassus who will stop at nothing to achieve his ends. Following his campaigns he brings back slaves to sell in Rome. After the wars in Thrace, those he brings back include Spartacus and his wife Phrygia. Spartacus is not used to slavery and determines to fight for his freedom.

The slave market takes place and Spartacus and Phrygia are separated. She has been bought by Crassus and taken to his villa in Rome. She is taunted about her capture by Aegina, who is Crassus's mistress, and forced to take part in an orgy for his friends. To amuse them further Crassus arranges a fight to the death between two blindfolded gladiators. Afterwards the winner takes off his mask. It is Spartacus and he is horrified at the thought of having killed another man.

He is sent back to the gladiators' quarters, where he calls on the others

---

Overleaf
Spartacus (Mikhail Lavrovsky) leads his troops into battle.

to break their chains and fight against their masters. They break free and escape to the countryside where they ask the peasants to join in their struggle for freedom. Soon they are joined by many other oppressed people until they grow into a huge army.

Spartacus is a natural leader, though he does not seek the post. He vows to lead this army of slaves to victory over the Romans and to release the thousands of other slaves. He also knows that he must find his beloved Phrygia.

He finds her in Crassus's villa and they are reunited while Crassus is busy entertaining rich noblemen with Aegina. As they enjoy themselves news is brought that the army of slaves is encircling the villa. They escape as best they can, leaving Spartacus in possession of the villa.

The army chase Crassus and capture him. They bring him before Spartacus who gives him the chance to save his life by fair combat. Spartacus defeats him, but instead of killing him allows him to go free.

Crassus swears he will take revenge for this humiliation and Aegina encourages him as she cannot bear to lose the power and riches Crassus has brought to her. She decides that she too will do all she can to take revenge on Spartacus.

At night she creeps into his camp where she is able to get advance news of his plans. She learns that not all of his commanders are as brave as he and that some feel that his plans are too dangerous to succeed.

While Spartacus and his loyal commanders await the renewed attack by Crassus, Aegina brings drink and women to tempt those weaker ones. She succeeds in distracting them and they fall to Crassus's stronger forces.

But Crassus knows that while Spartacus lives there will be trouble for the Empire and he will not rest till he is dead. He follows the remnants of Spartacus's army.

He succeeds in encircling Spartacus and his troops who are growing fewer and fewer. In spite of this, Spartacus fights back bravely, but he is caught in a clever ambush. As he dies a hero's death, the Romans lift him high on their spears. Phrygia finds the battlefield too late. She is heart-broken when she sees the broken body of her beloved Spartacus.

Opposite
Ekaterina Maximova and Vladimir Vasiliev in *Spartacus*.

Overleaf
Nadezhda Pavlova and Aleksandr Bogatyrev acknowledge the applause of a packed audience after a performance of *Giselle* at the Bolshoi Theatre, Moscow.

Glossary

Adage referring to the slow tempo either of an exercise in class, or the first part of a classical *pas de deux* in which the man partners the ballerina.
Allegro steps in fast tempo in class or during a ballet including the quick beaten steps.
Arabesque the position in which the dancer stands on one leg with the other stretched out at the back, with the arms arranged harmoniously. There are several different types depending on the position of the body, the height of the legs, or the position of the arms.
Attitude one of the most famous poses in the ballet when the dancer stands on one leg with the other raised to the back and bent at the knee. It can also be performed to the front. It is based on the statue of Mercury by Bologna.
Ballerina actually any female dancer, but now used to indicate a principal dancer.
Ballet blanc a 'white ballet' like *Les Sylphides* or the second act of *Giselle*, associated with the Romantic style.
Ballet d'action the first story ballets.
Ballet Master now the person who teaches the company and arranges and takes rehearsals. Originally the choreographer and creator of ballets.
Ballon the quality of 'bounce' in dancing.
Barre the wooden rail which dancers use for support during their classes. It is also the title of the part of the class during which they stand at it.
Battement the term used to describe the beating movements of the legs.
Batterie the term used to describe the steps in which the feet beat together or cross in the air.
Character Dancing dances which come from folk or national dances such as mazurkas or Neapolitan dances. The character dancer is someone who specializes in these lively dances or in playing very realistic parts.
Coda the last and very brilliant section of a classical *pas de deux*.
Corps de ballet the group of dancers who make up the ballet company,

from whom the soloists and principals will graduate.

Coryphée the first grade of soloist after *corps de ballet* level. A term still used by many classical companies.

Danseur noble a male dancer who is of the grand classical style and takes the parts such as Prince Siegfried or Albrecht. The equivalent, but not much used although there is no other, of the principal ballerina.

Demi-caractère refers to dancers who take roles such as Swanilda who combine the qualities of the ballerina and the character dancer.

Demi-plié a half-bend of the knees which is used as a preparation for take off and landing of jumps ensuring softness of landings. Also as a preparation to push off for turning.

Divertissement a ballet or part of a ballet which consists of separate dances which might be quite different or perhaps linked by a similar theme.

Elevation the dancer's ability to jump into the air and, if possible, give the brief illusion of staying still at the peak of a jump.

Enchâinement the combination of a sequence of steps to form a short dance.

Entrechat when the dancer jumps into the air and changes the position of the feet before landing. Each has a number depending on the number of changes, i.e., entrechat quatre, entrechat six.

Étoile a star dancer, particularly at the Paris Opéra.

Fouetté the fast turning movement when the ballerina (usually) raises one leg, bends it at the knee and uses a whipping movement to turn very quickly.

Jeté a jump. There are many different types.

Leotard the bathing-suit-like clothing which dancers wear.

Line the way the dance uses legs and arms in poses so that they all combine to form a harmonious and elegant picture.

Manège circling the stage with a particular step. The term originally came from the earliest horse ballets.

Mime telling the story of a ballet with gestures of the body. In modern ballets this is kept to a minimum.

Pirouette a complete turn of the body. There are many different types according to the position of the raised leg.

Plié bending the knees, slowly and evenly, whilst keeping the feet in one of the five positions, to warm the muscles. Most steps begin or end with a plié which helps the dancer to leave the ground and to make a soft landing.

Pointe the tip of the toe on which the ballerina learned to stand at the beginning of the nineteenth century.

Port de bras the way the arms are carried, as well as the positions of the arms during certain steps.

Positions the basic positions of the feet numbered from first to fifth.
Révérence a bow or curtsey at the end of the performance or by tradition at the end of a ballet class.
Spotting the technique of fixing the eyes on a spot, immediately to the front, to help turning.
Tights dance-wear from feet to waist.
Tour en l'air when the dancer jumps straight up into the air and performs one complete turn of the body, or more.
Turn-out the position of the feet, in line from toe through the heel and heel through to toe, so that the feet make a straight line.
Tutu a ballerina's dress, either long for the Romantic ballets, or shorter for the classical ballets.
Warm-up what every dancer must do before performing. A brief version of a ballet class to make sure the muscles are warm. Without it injuries are much more likely.

Ballet Time Chart

This is a list of some of the most important dates in the story of ballet from the time of early court entertainments. I have included some other important events so that you will have some idea of how the development of ballet fitted in with happenings of the time.

1581 On 15 October the *Ballet Comique de la Reine* is performed.

1605 Ben Jonson and Inigo Jones work on the brilliant *Twelfth Night Masque*.

1607 Production of Monteverdi's *Orfeo* which includes light ballet scenes.

1616 Death of William Shakespeare.

1620 Pilgrim Fathers settle in America.

1653 Louis XIV dances the role of the Sun King.

1653 Oliver Cromwell becomes Lord Protector in Britain.

1661 The Academy of the Dance is founded by Louis XIV.

1664 The English take New York from the Dutch.

1671 Beauchamps becomes Ballet Master to Louis XIV.

1696 Peter the Great becomes Tsar of Russia and encourages dancing.

1700 Beauchamps writes down the five positions of the feet.

1707 Marie Sallé the great ballerina is born.

1710 Marie-Anne de Cupis de Camargo, her great rival, is born.

1715 Death of Louis XIV.

1726 Marie de Camargo makes her début at the Paris Opéra.

1727 Jean-Georges Noverre, the great force in changing ballet, is born.

1729 Gaetano Vestris, the first great *danseur* is born.

1734 Marie Sallé appears in London wearing only a flimsy costume in *Pygmalion*, the first breakaway from heavy old-fashioned dresses.

1735 The Empress Anne opens the Imperial State Dancing Academy in St Petersburg.

1740 Frederick the Great becomes King of Prussia.

1748 The Royal Danish Theatre opens in Copenhagen.

1755 Noverre arranges dances for David Garrick, the great actor, in London.

1760 Noverre, in Stuttgart, begins work on his ideas for costume and character which will change ballet into a theatre art and which will be published as his *Letters*.
1766 *Pirouettes à la seconde* performed for the first time by Anna Heinel.
1769 The birth of Napolean Bonaparte.
1769 Salvatore Viganò, who would become an important teacher, is born.
1770 Captain Cook lands in Botany Bay.
1776 The American Declaration of Independence.
1778 First performance of the Mozart ballet *Les Petits Riens*.
1778 The opening of La Scala Opera House in Milan.
1786 *The Whims of Cupid*, by Galeotti, performed in Copenhagen where it is still in the repertoire.
1789 First performance of *La Fille Mal Gardée* by Dauberval.
1789 The French Revolution.
1792 *The Bird Catcher* danced in New York with John Durang the first American professional dancer.
1800 Electricity discovered by Alessandro Volta.
1801 *The Creatures of Prometheus*, Beethoven's only ballet, staged by Viganò in Vienna.
1805 Hans Christian Andersen born in Denmark.
1810 Fanny Elssler born.
1810 Jules Perrot, who with Jean Coralli would create *Giselle*, is born.
1815 The Battle of Waterloo.
1816 Antoine Bournonville, father of Auguste, becomes ballet master in Copenhagen.
1817 Fanny Cerrito is born.
1818 Marius Petipa, later creator of the classic ballets in St Petersburg, is born.
1819 Carlotta Grisi, the first Giselle, is born.
1819 Lucille Grahn, the Danish ballerina, is born.
1820 George IV, formerly Prince Regent, becomes King of Britain.
1820 Carlo Blasis's treatise on dance technique, still an important text-book today, is published.
1822 The first print made showing a dancer on point. She probably only stood on tip-toe for a fleeting moment.
1822 Gas lighting replaces candles and natural light at the Paris Opéra.
1825 Augusta Maywood, the first American ballerina, is born.
1825 The Bolshoi Theatre opens in Moscow.
1832 The first performance of *La Sylphide* at the Paris Opéra with Marie Taglioni as the Sylph.
1834 *La Sylphide* is shown in America for the first time.
1836 Auguste Bournonville, who succeeded his father as ballet master in

Copenhagen, creates his own version of *La Sylphide.*

1839 George Washington Smith, the first American *danseur noble*, makes his début.

1840 The birth of Peter Ilyich Tchaikovsky.

1841 The first performance of *Giselle.*

1842 The first performance of *Napoli* in Copenhagen.

1845 Texas joins the United States.

1845 The four great ballerinas of the age, Taglioni, Cerrito, Grahn and Grisi dance the *Pas de Quatre* in London.

1846 *Giselle* is staged in America for the first time.

1847 Marius Petipa goes to Russia after a career dancing in France.

1854 The Crimean War begins.

1858 The Royal Opera House in London reopens in the form it has today.

1860 The Maryinsky, now the Kirov, Theatre opens in St Petersburg.

1862 Marius Petipa has his first great success in Russia with *The Daughter of the Pharaoh.*

1865 The end of the American Civil War.

1866 The popular musical show *The Black Crook* opens in New York.

1870 The first performance of *Coppélia* by Saint-Léon in Paris.

1872 Serge Diaghilev is born.

1875 Paris Opéra opens in its present form.

1876 The invention of the telephone.

1876 The first performance of *Sylvia.*

1877 The first disastrous performance of *Swan Lake* in Moscow.

1878 Isadora Duncan is born. She would become a major influence in the forming of a Modern Dance movement.

1880 Mikhail Fokine is born.

1881 Anna Pavlova is born.

1883 The Metropolitan Opera House in New York opens.

1885 Virginia Zucchi, the Italian ballerina, dazzles Russia with her sparkling technique.

1890 The first performance of *The Sleeping Beauty* by Petipa.

1892 The first performance of *The Nutcracker* by Petipa and Lev Ivanov.

1893 Death of Tchaikovsky.

1893 Henry Ford makes his first car.

1895 The first production of *Swan Lake* by Petipa and Ivanov.

1898 Vaslav Nijinsky enters the Imperial Ballet School.

1899 Anna Pavlova makes her début at the Maryinsky Theatre, St Petersburg.

1899 Diaghilev and his collaborators start the magazine 'The World of Art' to put forward their ideas about ballet production.

1899 Isadora Duncan gives her first recital in Chicago.

1901 *Death of Queen Victoria.*

1902 Tamara Karsavina makes her début at the Imperial Theatre. She will go on to dance with Nijinsky and create many roles for Fokine.

1903 *The Wright brothers make the first flight in America.*

1907 Fokine creates *The Dying Swan* for Pavlova.

1909 Diaghilev's Russian Ballet gives its first season in Paris including Fokine's *Les Sylphides* created the year before.

1910 *Swan Lake* is presented in England for the first time at the London Hippodrome.

1910 The first performance of *The Firebird* with music by Igor Stravinsky.

1911 *Amundsen reaches the South Pole.*

1912 Nijinsky choreographs and dances *Afternoon of a Faun.*

1914 *The outbreak of the First World War.*

1915 Leonide Massine, after being the leading dancer, becomes choreographer for Diaghilev.

1916 The first American season of the Russian Ballet and Nijinsky dances there for the first time.

1917 *The Russian Revolution which cuts many dancers off from their homeland.*

1918 *The end of the Great War.*

1919 Nijinsky retires through mental ill health from which he never recovers.

1920 The Royal Academy of Dancing is founded in London.

1921 At the invitation of the Soviet Government Isadora Duncan tries to form a school in Russia.

1921 Diaghilev produces his very grand version of *The Sleeping Beauty* in London at the Alhambra Theatre, with disastrous financial results.

1921 Bronislava Nijinska, sister of Vaslav, becomes choreographer to Diaghilev.

1924 George Balanchine becomes choreographer to Diaghilev.

1926 *The General Strike in Britain as a result of social unrest.*

1926 Martha Graham gives her first solo recital in New York.

1926 Ninette de Valois founds her school in London.

1928 Balanchine creates *Apollo* to music by Stravinsky.

1928 Ninette de Valois's pupils dance at the Old Vic Theatre for the first time.

1929 *The Wall Street Crash.*

1929 The last performance by the Russian Ballet and the death of Diaghilev in Venice.

1930 Frederick Ashton produces his first ballet, *Capriol Suite*, for the Marie Rambert dancers, having previously contributed *A Tragedy of Fashion* to a revue in 1926.

1930 The American première of *The Rite of Spring* by Massine with Martha Graham as the Chosen Maiden.

1931 After a lifetime bringing ballet to every continent, Anna Pavlova dies in The Hague, Holland.

1931 The Vic-Wells Ballet, which will become the Sadler's Wells Ballet and eventually the British Royal Ballet, gives its first performance.

1933 Adolf Hitler comes to power in Germany.

1933 The first performances by *Les Ballets 1933* which show Balanchine's last ballets before he goes to America.

1933 George Balanchine and Lincoln Kirstein found the School of American Ballet.

1934 The first all-English production of *Giselle* by the Vic-Wells Ballet, with Alicia Markova in the title role. The same year saw the first *Swan Lake*, also danced by Markova.

1934 The School of American Ballet gives its first performances, including *Mozartiana* and *Serenade* by George Balanchine.

1936 The Ballet Club in London give the first performance of *Lilac Garden* the first of Antony Tudor's important ballets.

1936 Ballet Caravan is formed by Lincoln Kirstein, now Director of the New York City Ballet with George Balanchine.

1938 The first performance of *Billy the Kid* with choreography by Eugene Loring and music by Aaron Copland. The first successful ballet with an American theme.

1939 The outbreak of the Second World War.

1940 American Ballet Theater gives its first season in New York. Some ballets are staged by Mikhail Fokine, who died two years later.

1944 *Fancy Free*, Jerome Robbins' first ballet is staged by the American Ballet Theater. It is now danced by both that company and the New York City Ballet for which he made so many later successful works.

1945 The end of the Second World War.

1945 Roland Petit gives the first season of his *Ballets des Champs Elysées* in Paris.

1946 The Royal Opera House, Covent Garden, reopens after the war years with a performance of *The Sleeping Beauty* by the Sadler's Wells Ballet with Margot Fonteyn in the title role.

1948 The first performance given by the newly formed New York City Ballet.

1948 The Sadler's Wells Ballet produce *Cinderella* by Frederick Ashton, the first full-length English ballet. The title role was danced by Moira Shearer who gained great popularity with her role in the film *The Red Shoes*.

1949 The first New York season by the Sadler's Wells Ballet, which was a great success.

1950 The Korean War.

1950 Vaslav Nijinsky dies in London. He is now buried in Paris.

1950 The first season in London of the newly formed Festival Ballet by Alicia Markova and Anton Dolin.

1951 After an unfortunate Australian tour the Ballet Rambert return home to celebrate their twenty-fifth anniversary. The company was formed by Marie Rambert who encouraged many choreographers, such as Ashton and Tudor, and who is still active in its affairs, although past ninety.

1951 The National Ballet of Canada is formed, based in Toronto under the direction of Celia Franca.

1952 The first hydrogen bomb is exploded in America.

1952 Elizabeth II becomes Queen of England.

1953 The Royal Danish Ballet makes its first appearance outside Denmark when it dances at the Royal Opera House, Covent Garden, as part of the Coronation celebrations.

1954 A new culture hits the world. Bill Haley records 'Rock around the Clock' and the world starts rocking and rolling.

1956 The first foreign tour by the Bolshoi Ballet from Moscow, which introduced its very spectacular dancers, including Ulanova, Plisetskaya and Fadeyechev, to the West as well as the very large-scale productions.

1956 The smaller Robert Joffrey Ballet starts to give performances in America. After many ups and downs it is still active today.

1956 *Les Grands Ballets Canadiens* founded in Montreal, third Canadian classical dance company. The first, The Royal Winnipeg Ballet, had been formed as long ago as 1939.

1957 Formation of the Western Theatre Ballet in Bristol, England, by Elizabeth West and the choreographer Peter Darrell. This was to be an influential company before financial difficulties forced it to close. Its members went on to form the Northern Dance Theatre based in Manchester and the Scottish Ballet, which Darrell still directs.

1958 Jerome Robbins founds Ballets: USA which gives performances at the Spoleto Festival in Italy. For it, amongst other works, he mounts his version of *Afternoon of a Faun*.

1959 Maurice Béjart choreographs his version of *The Rite of Spring* in Brussels for a group of dancers which will become his company: the Ballet of the Twentieth Century.

1960 John Cranko is invited to Stuttgart to mount his ballet *The Prince of the Pagodas* and stays to found the very fine company which still exists there under the direction of his ballerina, Marcia Haydée.

1961 *Yuri Gagarin is the first man in space.*

1961 Rudolf Nureyev makes his 'leap for freedom' at Paris Airport. He becomes the biggest ballet personality in the world, together with Margot Fonteyn. Their partnership inspired Ashton to create *Marguerite and Armand* for them and their performances in classic ballets will always be remembered. Nureyev was the first star of the Kirov Ballet of Leningrad to leave, but he has since been followed by Natalia Makarova and Mikhail Baryshnikov.

1962 The formation of the Australian Ballet, now an important company with a fine repertoire and a school which supplies most of its dancers.

1963 *Beatlemania begins.*

1963 *The death of President Kennedy of the United States.*

1963 Frederick Ashton succeeds Ninette de Valois as Director of the British Royal Ballet. As her co-director and choreographer, he had created many wonderful ballets, including perhaps his most popular, *La Fille Mal Gardée* (1960).

1964 Merce Cunningham brings the company he founded in 1953 to Europe. His influence has grown enormously since then, and the collaborations with famous painters and musicians, such as Robert Rauschenberg and John Cage, have given many people new ideas about what dance should do.

1965 Kenneth MacMillan produces his first full-length ballet, *Romeo and Juliet.* Following this he went to Berlin to become director of the ballet there, before returning to London to become Director of the British Royal Ballet in 1970.

1966 The Ballet Rambert change direction and become a modern dance company. Since then their reputation has grown and they are now one of the most important companies in the world with fine dancers and a good repertoire.

1969 *American astronauts set foot on the Moon.*

1970 Martha Graham retires as a dancer after a career which has spanned over fifty years. During that time she influenced almost every living dancer and choreographer.

I will not extend this list, date by date, past this point. Of course many wonderful things have happened since then in the world of ballet, so many that the list would be almost endless. There have been hundreds of successful productions alone, but which will last and which will influence the next generation of dancers and choreographers, it is very difficult to tell.

Index of Ballets

Acknowledgments

The illustrations are reproduced by kind permission of the following: New York City Ballet page 3; Victoria and Albert Museum 6, 53; Craig Dodd (author's collection) 8, 9, 15, 64, 68, 72; Wallace Collection 10; Charles Tandy 11; Novosti Press Agency 13, 14 (left & right), 40, 43, 144–145, 146, 148; WNET/13 Costas, USA 16, 47; Colette Masson, Paris 17; Jesse Davis (Mike Davis Studios Ltd) 18, 25, 42, 46, 88, 120–121, 125, 126, 127, 130–131, 133; Anthony Crickmay 19, 22, 50, 67, 83, 112, 118; Andrew Oxenham (National Ballet of Canada) 21; Zoe Dominic 23; Leslie E. Spatt 27, 106, 140, 141; Martha Swope, New York 29; Tony van Muyden, The Hague 30; Don Edwards (Australian Information Service) 33; Malcolm Hoare 36, 37, 38, 39, 78; The Louvre, Paris 45; R. Kayaert, Brussels 49; Roger Wood 55; Chimera Foundation for Dance, Inc., New York 56; Enar Merkel Rydberg, Stockholm 59, 116; Houston Rogers 60–61; Karsten Bundgard 69; Stuart Robinson 70; Donald Southern 75, 77; Australian Ballet 79; National Ballet of Canada 80, 82; Heinz Köster, Berlin 89; Paramount Picture Corporation 94; Barry W. Gray (National Ballet of Canada) 100; William Cooper 109; Michael Richardson 136–137.

The author has made every effort to credit the illustrations correctly, but would be pleased to correct any errors in future editions.